An Unlikely & Reluctant Messenger

BOLANLE PACHECO

Dedication

To Abayomi (Mighty Joe) Pacheco
You've been my rock, sanity and ATM through this writing and figuring out ME process. I thank you for always believing in me and our relationship and always putting US first. You've been a great friend, lover and husband and I can't thank you enough for your patience and understanding. I thank Yahuah every day for blessing me with such a wonderful man; I can't imagine my life without you. I also want to thank you for being an EXCELLENT daddy to little Evan (I'm glad he has such a great role model to look up to in you). You and I together FOREVER baby. I love you with all my heart and being. Muah xoxo.

Acknowledgement

To my Saviour, Yeshua. Thank you for entrusting me to deliver this message.

To my baby boy Evan, thank you for always encouraging me with your "I'm so proud of you words." I love you.

I am thankful to have been blessed with an awesome support system in the form of my family, I could not have asked for a better set of parents (Anthony and Adijat Coker) and siblings (Sta Dupe, Sta Lola, Sta Shola, Sta Doyin, Bro. Ayotunde, Sta tinuke, Ayo, Kolade, Dami, Leke and Prince). Sta Dupe, Sta Shola, Sta Doyin and Sta Tinuke, thank you all for contributing to my growth and development and still treating me like the last born and giving me money when I need it. I hope you will never stop...lol. You are appreciated.

Daddy, thank you for being the best dad you could be. You're the world's best dad.

Mummy (Iya agba), what can I say about you, iya ni wura, thank you for being an excellent mother and going all out for all your children.

Sta Dupe, my angel on earth; thank you for always being humble, kind, generous, grounded and level-headed. We are blessed to have such a selfless being amongst us. Thank you for always being there for me

Sta Shola, my roll dog, if we weren't ten years apart, I would have sworn we were twins because we just gel and you get me. Thanks for being my accountability partner and always keeping me on track.

Sta Doyin, the fashionista and woman of God, thank you for training me in Yahuah's ways.

Sta Tinuke, the CEO and best godmother on earth, thank you for always being there for Evan and me, I know I can always count on you whenever I am in a jam. I'm truly blessed to call you a sister.

To Arc. Ayodele & Mrs. Olatunde Pacheco; thank you for birthing my Mr. Wonderful and raising him to be an excellent husband and father. I love you.

To Yetunde, my sister from another mother, thank you for always being there for me and cooking for me whenever you visit. I couldn't have asked for a better "younger" sister.

To my friend Sharon Hamilton who kept me in faith throughout this writing process, you are appreciated. Love you.

Progress is impossible without change, and those who cannot change their minds cannot change anything
~ George Bernard Shaw.

Contents

Appeal

I am a Stayhomepreneur i.e. a stay-at-home wife; mom and spiritual coach so please excuse my lack of writing professionalism. I have written this book, out of obedience to the Most High and not to impress people with my writing skills so please look past any grammatical, punctuation, or formatting issues you may find and FOCUS on the MESSAGE and not the noise around it.

You will notice I refer to 'God' as *YAHUAH*, His Hebrew name. He's commonly referred to as God or Lord because He is the Master of the Universe but those are titles. He has a name and He wants to be called by that name and not the titles we've been calling Him all these years. He tells us in Isaiah 42:8, saying, *"I am Yahuah that is my name! I will not give glory to anyone else, nor share my praise with carved idols....."* There are plenty gods out there and they BOW to Him. He doesn't want to share a name with them no matter how BIG we make the G. It's still the name *god*. Yahuah is the Creator of Heaven and this awesome world. He is not a god; He is *YAHUAH*! And so I have substituted the words *God* and *Lord* for Yahuah in most cases.

The same is the case with Jesus. We call Yeshua Jesus but just like Yahuah isn't going to share His glory or praise with anyone, Yeshua won't either! We have to call "Jesus" His Hebrew name, Yeshua and not the interpretation it turns out to be in the English language. No offense, but there are plenty people named Jesus running around that you can't liken to Yeshua, so they can't share His glory. While I'm on that topic, let's put this to rest right now. That white Jesus you see in pictures, maybe on your wallpapers, stickers and calendars, is NOT Yeshua; please stop circulating that image. Revelations 1:13-14 tells us "His head and his hairs were white like wool, as white as snow; and his eyes were as a flame of fire as white as snow {not Caucasian; Revelation 14:22} and his arms and his feet like in colour to polished brass {Darker skinned, not Caucasian; Daniel 10:6}." So can we let that "Jesus" picture rest right with the name and move ahead with YESHUA. These names sound weird at first and it will take some time to get used to them but as you continue to read, you'll get used to it.

This book has three parts: My Background Story - how I started in life and transitioned through many phases until God conquered me, then it progresses to the "Messages" and finally the prophesy about Nigeria I've received from the Holy Spirit in spite of the fact I'm 'not worthy,' thus proving Yahuah is using a 'foolish' vessel to pass a word to the wise, and a 'weak' person to daze the strong.

PS: I borrowed a lot of work from several sources e.g. books, quotes, songs, etc. and I did my best to acknowledge the true owners but in the event I've left some off please know it was not intentional and you can contact me so I can make the correction in subsequent editions. Thanks

My Intention with this Book

This book was written to share the Good News about Yahuah and His Kingdom using His Word {Bible}, as well as my life experiences in the hopes that it will be beneficial to somebody in this journey we call *life*. I will also attempt to reiterate principles in the Bible that we may have tainted, neglected or abused in today's Christendom.

I have done my best to recreate events, locations, and conversations from my memories. But in order to maintain anonymity, in some instances, I have changed the names of individuals and places. It is not my intention to paint any "character" in this book in a bad light, but it is inevitable as I am telling my story as I experienced it. If any of the people I wrote about happen to read this book, please know this is not shade (even though I might throw one or two. Ha-ha); it is the reality I lived.

What I intend for this book is that it will help change peoples' thinking and renew their minds which will, in turn, change their lives for the better and I decree and declare that when people see, hear, touch and/or read this book, they will receive an INSTANT miracle. Yes, I know it sounds too good to be true, and it may very well be, but only the strength of your faith will determine that. Speaking on the strength of faith, let's take a look in the Bible at the "woman with the issue of blood." In Mark 5: 25-34, we find that she is one person who had unbelievable faith and walked by it, instead of letting her situation determine her walk.

Let's look more closely at her story. She had been sick for 12 years, had spent all her money on doctors but was not only still sick, she was worse off. She had most likely been told she would be that way for the rest of her life, living with the bad condition, but when she heard about Yeshua, she became full of hope. I've tried to imagine all that transpired when she decided to go out to meet Yeshua for her miracle. She thought to herself, "I've got to meet Him because I know I will be healed." A flow of fear rushed over her when she stepped outside of her door to go find Yeshua as she was not supposed to be out at that time of the day because she was considered unclean. She dismissed the fear because the outcome *she was expecting* exceeded the risks. She got to the square and noticed Yeshua was done teaching and moving on to His next destination with crowds of people around Him. Doubt and worry crept in and she thought, "I'm too late; there's no way I'm going to get to Him, let me head back home," but courage overtook her, and instead she thought, "I've made it this far; it's all or nothing." She started pushing her way through the crowd, and as she was getting closer, she realised she wouldn't need to get His attention, and touching would be enough for her miracle, *"FOR SHE SAID*, 'If I may touch but his clothes, I shall be whole.'" She reached for the hem of His garment, and we know how the story ends. She touched the garment and as soon as she did, she was healed and made whole.

My question to you: Do you have that kind of faith? That deep-rooted, unshaken faith; the kind of faith that brings miracles. Yahuah wants to change our situation even more than we do, but He can't do anything in our lives if we don't have faith. Hebrews 11: 6 says, *"But without faith it is impossible to please him: for him that cometh to Yahuah **must believe** that he is, and that he is a rewarder of them that diligently seek him."* In other words, it is impossible to please Yahuah without faith. Anyone who wants to come to Him must believe that Yahuah exists and that He rewards those who sincerely seek Him. This is Yahuah telling us what we *must* do to be a member of His Kingdom. We have to have faith, because without faith, Yahuah cannot move in our lives and if He cannot move in our lives, He can't influence the people around us. He also tells us in 2 Corinthians 1:20, *"For all the promises of Yahuah in him are yea, and in him Amen, unto the glory of Yahuah by us."* Everything we ask Him for, as long as it is within the confines of His commandments, will be **DONE! :)**

There has been a stagnation of miracles in Yahuah's Kingdom on earth, and it's not because Yahuah stopped performing miracles. No, not at all. It's because we stopped believing and having faith! Before Yeshua left the earth, He said in Mark 16:15-18, *"Go ye into all the world, and preach the gospel to every creature. He that believeth and is baptized shall be saved; but he that believeth not shall be damned. And these signs shall follow them that believe: in my name they shall cast out devils, they shall speak with new tongues, they shall take up serpents; and if they drink any deadly thing, it shall not hurt them; they shall lay hands on the sick and they shall recover."* Yeshua also says in John 10:10b, *"I am come that they might have life, and that they might have it more abundantly."* Most of us, however, are not living abundantly i.e. abundance of grace from Christ, spiritual blessing, fullness of joy, glory, happiness, divine health etc. instead we are stressed, diseased, broken, hurting and sometimes even worse off than an unbeliever. It shouldn't be so.

Yahuah's Kingdom is a Kingdom of abundance in every aspect and facet, whether it concerns health, mental, spiritual, economical, and even sexual matters {meaning sex between married couples should be satisfying}. While everything won't be perfect because unwholesome life circumstances always sometimes come in to meddle with our affairs, we are still covered as Yahuah always cushions our blows and He gives us a sure fire way to rise above those circumstances. Yeshua tells us in Mark 11:23-24, *"'For verily I say unto you, that whosoever shall say unto this mountain, Be thou removed, and be thou cast into the sea; and shall not doubt in his heart, but shall believe that those things which he saith shall come to pass; he shall have whatsoever he saith."* If only we would have faith and believe Yahuah's word, we would live heavenly lives on earth.

Please join me in prayer:

Dear Yahuah, we come to you in the name of Almighty Yeshua and ask that you open the eyes of our heart so we can walk by faith. I pray that everyone, whose eyes, ears and hands are exposed to this book, will receive an instant MIRACLE. I take authority over every stronghold the devil has over the individual exposed to this book and I release him/her from it. I command the angels to go forth and assist them in every and any situation they need help with. I break any generational curses and cast down every work of the enemy in his/her life. I speak supernatural generational blessings, divine health {physical and mental}, divine healing and favour so he or she can advance and be a blessing to Your Kingdom. I speak it, believe and receive it in Yeshua's name. Amen.

PS: Some will consider this a "name it and claim it" approach. Call it what you want, but this is how Yahuah's Kingdom works. IT IS A LAW! This is why Yahuah spoke when He created the earth and the Holy Spirit went to work (more on this later). The Bible tells us in Proverbs 18:21, *"Death and life are in the power of the tongue: and they that love it shall eat the fruit thereof."* The words that come out of our mouths literally create our reality, so we need to make sure we are speaking the right things with that said, I can't also ignore the fact that people have abused this principle and expect Yahuah to act like a genie. Nevertheless, it doesn't negate the fact that speaking things into existence is one of the instruments used in Yahuah's

Kingdom. It just has to be done within Yahuah's will. I suggest you start speaking out your 'miracle', thank Yahuah continually in advance for it, and believe you've received it in the name of Yeshua Christ and you will have it. "There is a miracle in your mouth" ~ John Osteen. Rise up and claim it!

Introduction

I never exactly made a book. It's rather like taking dictation. I was given things to say.
~C. S. Lewis

I once heard a story about Truth and Lies. They went swimming one day and as they were swimming, Lies jumped out of the water, put on Truth's clothes and took off running. After a while, Truth came out of the water; realizing Lies took off with his clothes. He took chase after Lies but till this day, Naked Truth has been trying to catch up to a Well-Dressed Lie. While you may not agree with everything or anything I write, my hope is that when you run into Naked Truth and a Well-Dressed Lie, you will be able to distinguish the clothes belonging to Naked Truth because he has receipts and Well-Dressed Lie doesn't.

***

I have been accused of being legalistic because I believe in Yahuah's Love as well as his WRATH and I don't believe being under His grace means we are free to do whatever we want; we must adhere to His commands even if they are from the Old Testament. Hebrews 10:26-31 (NLT) tells us " *Dear friends, if we deliberately continuing sinning after we have received knowledge of the truth, there is no longer any sacrifice that will cover these sins. There is only the terrible expectation of Yahuah's judgment and the raging fire that will consume his enemies. For anyone who refused to obey the Law of Moses was put to death without mercy on the testimony of two or three witnesses. Just think how much worse the punishment will be for those who have trampled on Yahuah's son, and have treated the blood of the covenant, which made us holy, as if it were common and unholy, and have insulted and disdained the Holy Spirit who brings Yahuah's mercy to us. For we know the one who said, 'I will take revenge. I will pay them back.' He also said, 'Yahuah will judge his own people.' It is a terrible thing to fall into the hands of Yahuah.*" At the end of the day, we have to ask ourselves and answer this critical question: Do we want to honour Yahuah and worship Him the way He wants, or do we want to honour Him the way we want and expect Him to accept it? In the words of Paul Washer (Sermonizer), "You may say, 'Yahuah doesn't hate anybody. Yahuah is love.' No, my friend. You need to understand something. Yeshua taught, the prophets taught, the apostle taught this: that apart from Yahuah's grace revealed in Christ Yeshua, the only thing left for you is the wrath, the fierce anger of Yahuah because of your rebellion and your sin."

***

Like C.S. Lewis, I can't exactly say I wrote this book; it was more of me being given the things to write—from reading Scripture, hearing that still small voice inside of me, famous quotes, books, images, songs, and pretty much whatever conveyed the message the Holy Spirit was sending me. The first time the Holy Spirit revealed the idea of this book to me, I literally had a panic attack. My breath quickened, my palms went clammy, and I started to sweat all over. I knew what Yahuah wanted me to do and there was no way to hide from it. I, however, rationalised it and chalked it all off to stress. As time went on, all I heard or saw was about writing a book and, at the same time, nothing really seemed to work out in my career any longer.

One day shortly after that, I picked up my Bible to read, something I hardly ever did back then, and I landed on the story of Jonah. For those who don't know the story, here's a summary. Yahuah gives Jonah an assignment to warn the people of Nineveh to turn from their evil ways, but Jonah does not want to go. So he boards a boat heading the opposite direction from Nineveh. Of course, nothing goes right after that. Yahuah sends a great wind on the sea, which makes the sea stormy to the point of the ship being in danger of breaking apart and sinking. Jonah fesses up and tells the sailors the seas are raging because of him, so they end up throwing him overboard. Immediately, the storm stops and the seas are calm again. Jonah gets swallowed by a big fish, but does not die and for three days, he sits in the belly of the fish. When Jonah realised there's no running from his purpose, he prays to Yahuah and asks for forgiveness for being disobedient. Yahuah forgives him by speaking to the fish and asking the fish to spit him out onto dry land. Jonah gets spit onto dry ground, and he goes and carries out his purpose.

Now whether the story of Jonah and the fish is true does not matter neither is it up for debate; the moral of Jonah's story is, we cannot hide from Yahuah and our purpose. What Yahuah wishes to accomplish through us will come to pass, no matter how much we fight it. Ephesians 2:10 tells us, *"For we are his workmanship, created in Christ Yeshua unto good works, which Yahuah hath ordained that we should walk in them."* Yahuah has ordained each and every one of us for a purpose, and He will see to it that we uphold those plans.

I knew Yahuah was talking to me and there was no hiding from my purpose, so I did the sensible thing—I stopped fighting and surrendered. At this point, I figured everything would be a walk in the park since I was now being obedient. Oh, how wrong I was! The negative circumstances, worry, doubts, condemnation, and every other negative emotion surfaced. I would have moments where I felt disqualified because I'm not the "perfect" Christian and don't have a perfect walk, and let's not even talk about the many things that have happened in my life that I'm not proud of. I have, however, come to understand how the Most High I serve works. 1 Samuel 16:7 tells us, *"But Yahuah said unto Samuel, 'Look not on his countenance, or on the height of his stature; because I have refused him: for Yahuah seeth not as man seeth; for man looketh on the outward appearance, but Yahuah looketh on the heart.'"* When I look further at the type of people Yahuah used in the past, I know I'm in good company: "Jacob was a cheat, Peter had a temper, David was an adulterer, Noah got drunk, Jonah ran from Yahuah, Paul was a murderer, Gideon was insecure, Miriam was a gossip, Martha was a worrier, Thomas was a doubter, Sarah was impatient, Elijah was depressed, Moses stuttered, Zacchaeus was short, Abraham was old, Lazarus was dead... "Yahuah doesn't call the qualified, He qualifies the called" (mybible.com). Yahuah has reminded me and continues to bring to mind that He uses ordinary people, like you and me, to do extraordinary things.

There is, however, a misconception that if Yahuah calls you or you are a follower of Christ, it means you are perfect and no longer sin. While that is the goal, Yahuah does not expect us to be perfect. He does, however, expect that we make a conscious effort to die to sin daily. I've realised Yahuah saw and sees something I didn't see in myself which is why He chose me to deliver this message and that's good enough for

me. I pray it will be good enough for you, too, so you can carry out whatever purpose Yahuah has put in you that you may have been putting aside because you don't think you're good enough.

PART 1

My Background

Chapter 1

Life Stinks

We are all a little broken, and that's okay ~ Unknown

Anyone who knows me knows I have been blessed with an illustrious and wonderful husband, topped with an all-round happy and intelligent son. We live an almost perfect life, but, as we all know, life is never perfect.

Early Years

I was born and raised in Eric Moore Towers in Lagos, Nigeria, the last of five girls—Moroun, Sade, Dotun, Titi and myself, Bolanle—in a situation most people would call dysfunctional.

My dad is a Christian and my mom was born a Muslim but embraced Christianity when she married my dad. I really didn't understand either religion; I just knew I liked going to both church and mosque. I particularly liked hearing the call to prayer coming from the mosque and the going up and down during the prayers. By the time I was three, my parents were separated and my dad also had another family. Being in a country like Nigeria, my dad ended up getting custody of us. This was *not* because my mom was incompetent, but because as we all know, in Nigeria, what the man says is king (well at least back then in the 80's), so it was no surprise my sisters and I ended up with my dad.

To make matters worse, my dad forbade my mom from coming to visit us inside the home, but we were allowed to visit with her outside the compound which meant we were out in the open and people would see us and shake their heads at us in pity. Being a child, I saw things through those eyes, and I couldn't for the life of me understand why my dad was always so mean to my mom. While I can't particularly say I loved my mom at this point in my life, what I did have for her was admiration and empathy anger so I started disliking my dad.

Mom's Poverty

My mom was poor, and I knew I didn't want to live that life. I hated going to visit her because of where she lived. She lived in Ijeshatedo, which I considered as low-class. To make matters worse, she lived in what we Nigerians call a "face me I face you" (See picture below). Once you stepped through the exterior door of the building, you walked into a dark corridor with a bit of light coming through the makeshift concrete window. A few steps past the window and to the right was my mother's room. There wasn't much to see, as it was a dark, tiny studio-sized room with no windows. There was stuff everywhere because she literally had to cramp all her earthly possessions into this box she called home. The only light in the room came from a dim, open-roped lamp hanging from the ceiling over her bed. Through the mesh of her mosquito net, I could always see her *Bibeli Mimo* (Yoruba Bible) and Quran placed on her pillow. (The funny thing is, now that I think about it, I always slept soundly whenever I slept on that bed.) There was no real kitchen; what served as a kitchen was an open space outside with firewood as the stove.

The exterior of my mother's "face me I face you" residence was even worse; it was filthy. I remember the first time I had to use the bathroom. My mom told me it was behind the house, so I stepped into the dark corridor and made my way to the *shalanga* (outhouse). I expected it to be dark outside, but the moon was a great source of light. When I saw the bathroom "door," I stopped in my tracks and was immediately sick to my stomach. The steel and wood contraption they used as a door was rusted, the wood was worn out probably from all the water from the *shalanga*, and there were old poop stains on the make-shift door. Yuck, yuck, yuck! I debated turning around and not going through with this, but I really needed to go, so I braved it.

Bolanle Pacheco

I slowly opened the door with two of my fingers and stuck my head in—lo, there was poop everywhere and it looked like the flies were having a party. I could feel myself throw up in my mouth, it was so disgusting! I turned around and I suddenly didn't have to go anymore. *I don't have to put up with this*, I thought to myself. *I have it good at home.* At my dad's house, we had everything we wanted: money, maids, drivers, clean bathrooms and freedom to do whatever it is we wanted. I stormed back into her room and asked why she lived in such a filthy place. She burst out crying, and I knew I had said the wrong thing. I felt so bad but even with making her cry, I told her I was ready to go because I didn't like the environment. She got me and my sister, Titi, ready and dropped us back at my dad's house. As time went on, I realised I had to get used to my mom's living situation because it wasn't going to change anytime soon. I trained myself to hold my #2's, so I wouldn't have to use that nasty outhouse and just peed outside like everyone else did.

What I remember vividly about my childhood was crying. My mom cried ALL the time because she wanted to be with us and she couldn't. Whenever we were allowed to spend the night with her, we could hear her crying late at night when she thought my sisters and I were asleep. I hated every minute of it.

Restaurant on Wheels

What I did love and looked forward to was helping her out with her restaurant-on-wheels business. Yes, restaurant-on-wheels! My mom was and is still very street-smart, so even though she found herself in a situation she probably never envisioned, she didn't become a victim and always kept pushing. She had a white Peugeot 404 pick-up truck which broke down most of the time (it was the only thing my dad let her keep when he asked her to move out). So guess what she did? She turned the pick up into a restaurant. While she didn't make much from the restaurant-on-wheels business, she made enough to live day to day. We would drive into Isolo, Lagos early in the morning around 8 a.m., park in front of Five Star Textile Mill, and start cooking in order to have the food ready right around lunchtime. The textile workers expected us to be there and would all come out to buy food from us. We had a regular menu of rice, beans, plantain, Eba, Okro, Amala, efo, fish and meat. Some customers would buy "take out", some would sit outside to eat their meal, and some would sit in the pick-up truck. We had two benches in the truck, one opposite the other, seating a total of six people. I would constantly hear people whispering to each other, asking why Dr. Coker's wife was selling food out of her truck, I started wondering the same thing, and I disliked my dad even more. Things continued like this for a while until my dad found out we were helping my mom, and he made her stop taking us with her because he didn't want his kids out there selling food.

We still visited with her outside the compound so people felt sorry for my mom, and they let her know it but that did nothing more than make my mom feel even worse about her situation.

Things went on like this for a couple of years, and by the time I was eight, my older sister Sade moved to the United States. My mother knew she had to do something different about her situation, or she would live out the rest of her life like that but she wanted something more than that out of life. She made the tough decision to move to the United States to be with my sister so she could start a better life for herself. By the time I was ten, she made the move.

Lessons Learnt

For the longest time, I blamed the "death" of my parents' marriage on my dad because all I saw was my mom's pain. As I got older, however, I realised that my mom was not without fault, and they both contributed to the demise of their marriage. My dad was hurt, too, and that hurt translated into how he treated her. I thank Yahuah for unanswered prayers because if He had answered them all, my dad would have been dead, and I would not have gotten the chance to get to know him and outgrow my dislike for him. I learnt from my experience how imperative it is for parents to talk to their children about their separation/divorce (no matter how young they might be) that way, the children don't form their own opinions on the situation wrongly and choose sides.

My parent's separation had a negative toll on us as children born out of their union as it sometimes made life unbearable for us. Parents should be aware that their children will be affected by whatever decisions—bad or good—they make in life.

Eric Moore Towers {Block C}

Picture of a typical "face me I face you

What a Peugeot 404 looks like – My mom turned hers into a restaurant on wheels

Picture from http://www.delest.nl/

Chapter 2

Misunderstood "Black Sheep"

To be great is to be misunderstood
~ Ralph Waldo Emerson

I was fourteen and practically living without rules because my dad had moved to Abuja (another state) for work, leaving my then seventeen-year-old sister Titi, twenty-two-year-old cousin Seye, and me alone at home (although technically he left us in the care of my older sister Moroun who had just gotten married and lived down the street from us). My sister Dotun was in college in Calabar, another state. Because I was from a broken home (as people referred to us back then), I found myself looking for love outside my family.

I was having fun and loving my freedom. Looking back, I can see now the freedom I had was both a gift and a curse. On the positive side, it made me independent at a very young age, as I learned to cook at eight years old and could take care of myself. On the other hand, I started dating, fell in love, and tried sex younger than I would have liked (15 if you're wondering). I liked boys and the attention I got from them and because I was a "tomboy," I had *a lot* of them as friends. It didn't help matters that I had a mind of my own and did whatever I wanted to do regardless of others' opinions. What I didn't factor in as a child was consequences: I didn't know my decisions would lead me down a path of what I used to call back then my *living hell*.

Labelled a Slut
Most days after school, I would hang out with my friends, guys and girls, but mostly guys, so I got labelled a slut by both the adults and kids in the area. The sad thing is at this point I wasn't even engaging in any slutty acts and even when I started dating my boyfriend (Tunde) I kept it on the low because even I knew fourteen was too young to have a boyfriend but that didn't last too long because it came out in the open and it didn't help my reputation. It was so horrible, parents would tell their kids not to hang out with me because I would "corrupt" them (funny thing is, most of these "good" kids either ended up getting pregnant really early, being "runs" girls or having shotgun weddings; anyway, I digress). Two boys in particular would yell and say nasty things about me. Soon enough, some

of the boys I thought were my friends started making up stories about having had sex with me.

One day, I walked out of my house and on the wall to my left in huge letters written with charcoal was "Bola is a slut." I didn't know what to do. I started frantically using my palms to wipe it off till I looked at the next wall and it was all over it, too. I knew it was a lost cause, so I stopped and continued to walk down the stairs and all I saw were more hateful things written about me. I held my head high and kept walking towards the entrance gate. As I was about to walk out, I heard someone yell, "Bola, you're a slut." I turned around and didn't see anyone; I didn't even know when the tears started flowing. I ran back home and cried my eyes out. Unfortunately, I didn't know this was the beginning of several years of torture.

I had some idea of why this was happening, but I sure didn't understand it. Yes, I had a boyfriend and while we had started kissing, that was all we were doing. I knew I wasn't supposed to be doing this, but how many kids out there at that age weren't doing the same thing? Just because I had the freedom and balls to do whatever I wanted to do didn't mean I was sleeping with any of the guys, at least that was my reasoning then. I realised quickly people's opinion of me were not going to change, so I learned to deal with it, not crying or losing sleep over it.

Acting Like I Don't Care

I believe this was the time I started to build my "I don't care demeanour." I knew what I was and was not doing, so I chose to "do me" and act as if I didn't care, even though it hurt when I heard rumours and the things people said about me. I figured I could either become a victim, try to change people's opinion of me, or just keep being *me*. I opted for the latter. I stopped hiding my relationship and decided that people would see me for who I really was. Although I had hoped this would make things better, this did nothing but make things worse but I no longer cared at that point.

Tunde, the First Love

During the first two years of dating Tunde, the relationship seemed great. He was a good guy, and no one could have told us we weren't going to get married. We were so sure of it; we always talked about the future, kids and the whole *shebang*. Suddenly, he stopped coming around as frequently and Tosan, the neighbourhood snitch as people used to refer to him back then, came to me and told me Tunde was cheating on me with another girl who lived down the street. I didn't believe him, so he offered to take me to see for myself. I took the bait and as we were walking there all I could do was pray that Tunde wouldn't be there. But that prayer wasn't answered because he was there. I was devastated; I thought our relationship was solid.

Someone must have told Tunde I was outside because he came rushing out as I started walking away. He tried to convince me that there was nothing going on, and he was just there visiting a friend. I wasn't ready to hear it and dismissed him. I went back home and started balling my eyes out. I heard a knock on my door and when I opened it, it was Tosan, coming to "console" me and before I knew what was going on, he kissed me and I kissed him back. I knew it wasn't right, but I did it anyway (another bad move on my part, I must say) by the following week, everyone and their momma knew I had kissed Tosan. This just gave people more ammunition to talk about me, especially since Tosan went around telling people he had slept with me. Tunde knew the truth and somehow we were able to get our relationship back on track.

My dad would come back home every Friday, and I believe he started hearing whispers of everything going on. By this time, I was sixteen. I figured since I had stopped hiding my boyfriend from others for a while now, it was time I introduced Tunde to my dad. It was a ballsy move, but I figured if he were going to have any crazy opinions about me, it would be for me having a boyfriend at a young age and nothing else. I introduced Tunde to my dad who welcomed him with open arms. We were both on a high that my dad accepted him until two days later when Tunde found out he was travelling to America. We were devastated. We couldn't believe it. What would happen to us? Would our relationship survive? We decided we would keep dating long distance, so he introduced me to his family. This didn't really matter, though, because everything happened so fast that about a week later, he was gone. Tunde moved out of the country to America.

Long-Distance Dating

Although Tunde and I had agreed to date long-distance, I was now alone, lonely and the target of some guys, even Tunde's friends. After all, the "slut" was single and they wanted to date her. My long distance relationship with Tunde went well in the first six months but slowly, the calls and the letters dwindled on both sides. Ten months later, I started dating someone else and a month into that relationship, he moved to London so here I was back to square one. I cried my eyes out because ten months before that, my first boyfriend Tunde had moved to the United States and now a month into a new relationship, my new boyfriend had moved to London.

I kept asking myself, "What the heck is going on here? On one of those "crying my eyes out days," I was on my bed doing just that while my then best friend Teniola and her boyfriend Biodun were in the room consoling me. Unbeknownst to us, my dad and his brother were knocking at the door and we didn't hear them. They must have been at the door for about thirty minutes before we finally answered the door. Can you imagine the shock on their faces when I opened the door and there stood the three of us? Can you say ménage a trois? My friends left and my dad said to me in a stern voice, "You really need to change; if you get pregnant, I will reap that baby out of you with a hanger and send you to a convent so you can become a nun." I wanted to tell him he had misunderstood what he thought he saw, but there was no use trying to convince him; he already believed what he wanted, so I just carried on my life as usual.

Fact to Note
Your true identity is not a function of what people say about you or your circumstances.

Chapter 3

Kissing Frogs

Sometimes you have to kiss a few frogs before finding Prince Charming ~ Unknown

Leke, the Romantic Hottie

I was reeling from my loss of yet another relationship and because I was always looking for love, life without a boyfriend was not working for me. Fast-forward a couple of months later, I was buying *Suya* when I turned around and there he was. I literally had to do a double take because he was so good looking. Instantly, I knew I had found my next boyfriend. He was there with one of his friends who happened to be someone I knew. This made things better because I knew how to find him. Everything in me wanted to speak to him, but I had to keep my cool and act like a lady, all the while praying he would say something to me. He didn't. I got my *Suya* and went home, but I couldn't stop thinking about him. Determined to see him again, I started plotting how I could make our meeting happen.

I woke up the next morning still trying to figure out how to see him again but around 1 p.m. guess who was at my house with his friend? Leke! The Law of the Universe, specifically, the Law of Attraction was at work or maybe I should I say I believed it with my heart and it happened. He introduced himself, and we talked for hours. While we were talking, he asked me to be his girlfriend. I guess you could say it was love at first sight for both of us. Leke was a really great boyfriend, he treated me like a queen, and we dated for about two years. We also knew without a doubt we were getting married, but things changed when we both started college. I was accepted into University of Abuja while he was accepted into Lagos State University. When I went back home for the holidays, I started hearing whispers about him seeing a girl in the neighbourhood. I was devastated but decided to find out if it was true or not since he denied it. I went over to her house, and I won't say she was surprised to see me. It was as if she had expected it. I asked her if it was true they were dating, and she said, "Yes." Surprisingly, I really wasn't upset because deep down, I already knew. Rather than flipping out on her, I calmly told her we were still dating, and that was when I knew he had lied to her about us still being together. Apparently, he had told her we had broken up due to the distance and were now just friends. Ouch!

Trying to Find Out the Truth

After going straight to his house to confront him, the first thing I said to him was, "Guess where I am coming from?" He didn't respond, so I told him. I could literally see all the blood drain from his face and the "I done messed up look" took over. I told him all I found out from her. He begged, pleaded, and told me he was going to break things off with her. Being young and in love, I asked him to go to her house right away and break up with her. So we drove to her house and he told her things were over between them. However, things were never the same with us. I couldn't trust him and once it was time to go back to college, we broke up.

Experiences in America

By the time I turned nineteen, my life had changed drastically. I was in a different college full time, had a full time job and my own apartment in AMERICA! It was like day and night; everything had changed and my "rich daddy girl" days were long over. I remember the days leading to my sister Titi and I leaving Nigeria. My dad sat me down and gave me a pep talk; he wanted to be sure I was ready to leave Nigeria. He explained how independent I would have to be because he wouldn't be there to provide for me. I told him I was up for the challenge and not to worry about me. Boy, I was up for a challenge!

The first day we got to the United States, my mom pretty much told my sister and me we had to get jobs. *Really? We've barely dropped our bags and you're already talking about a job?* We thought she was joking till we asked her for some money to do some shopping. When she handed us only $50 bucks each, we knew she meant business. We got with the programme really quickly. By the following week, we both had jobs at a telemarketing firm making $6.50 an hour and were bumped up to $7.00 by the following week.

I liked the laid-back environment at work and enjoyed working with a bunch of young adults still trying to find themselves, just like me. However, Titi and I didn't know what we had signed up for especially since we didn't have telemarketers in Nigeria. Because we had just come into the country, our accents were still really "thick," and customers were rude and mean. Someone actually told me, "Go, call your own f$%#king country and stop calling here with that f%$#ed up accent." This became a common occurrence. Titi and I decided this wasn't the job for us, so we started looking for other jobs. About a month later, we found jobs at the Christiana Mall in Newark, DE. I got a job at Strawbridge's making $7.50 an hour while Titi got a job at Aeropostale making $8.00 an hour. After working at the mall for a couple of months, we both knew it was time to go. By March 2001, the following year, Titi and I were both working at call centres as customer service reps making $10.50 and $10.35 an hour respectively. We felt we had arrived, living the American Dream, and *no one could tell us nothing!*

By August 2001, I had settled in to life in America and knew it was time to buy a car; catching the bus was becoming exhausting. I was lucky enough to have a mama with really good credit and a willingness to co-sign a loan for me. I bought a green 1997 Saturn S series with a monthly payment of $119. *Ahhh! Life was good; no more catching the bus. Whoop whoop!*

Grayson, the Responsible Bad Boy

I had my routine down—college, work, and home—and this continued for about a year. One fateful day during the spring of 2002, I was driving home from my sister Sade's house. I was at a red light bumping some music in my car and dancing when I felt someone watching me. I looked to my right, and there was a guy looking and smiling at me. He said something but I didn't hear him, so he asked that I roll down my window. I obliged and he said something to the effect of it 'seeming like I didn't have a care in the world.' We started making small talk and didn't realise the light had changed to green till the cars behind us started to blare their horns. He asked me to pull over which I did (I know, I know he could have been a serial killer and all, but I was young and all I saw was his cuteness), lol.

When we both got out of our cars, the first thing he said was, "You're cute." I started grinning from ear to ear. He told me his name was Grayson, and I told him my name was Bola. He said, "That's different; where are you from?" I told him Africa, Nigeria to be precise. He got excited and said, "A real African queen!" While I knew he was running game on me, I still liked that he said it. He asked me where I was off to, and I told him I was heading home. I asked him the same question, and he said he was off to pick up his son...*womp, womp, womp.* That was a total turn off for me because I had sworn *never* to date a guy with kids, as I didn't want to deal with any baby-mama drama. He must have noticed the look on my face had changed when he said that, so he shared that he was a single dad because his fiancée had passed away. Thus, there wouldn't be any baby-mama drama. I figured I could make an exception since I wouldn't have to deal with any drama. I gave him my number and headed on my merry way.

Grayson called me about thirty minutes later, and we talked for a long time. I found out his fiancée had passed away from lupus a year or so ago and he was raising his son, even though his fiancée's mother had offered to help raise him. I had so much respect and admiration for him because you typically hear about the guys who don't want to have anything to do with their kids. He told me he worked in construction which was initially a turn-off, especially since this type of job was for people on the bottom of the totem pole in Nigeria (at least, this is what I thought). But he was cute and responsible (He had to be since he was taking care of his son, right?), so I decided to see where this could go.

We talked on the phone a lot and soon started dating. A couple of weeks into dating, I met his mom and son. She was extremely nice and his son was so adorable that I immediately fell in love with him. When I was leaving, I heard his mom say to him, "I like her; she's not like that crazy one." I wondered what she meant, but figured she was referring to his son's mom. This didn't really add up, though, because from what I had heard about her, she was nothing short of an angel, but I didn't give it much thought.

The Truth Comes Out

A few months into dating, I noticed I never really saw Grayson go to work. Also, for a construction worker, his phone rang *a lot*. I asked him about his work situation, and he explained he was on break. That didn't make a lot of sense to me since it was summer, typically the busiest months for contractors. I shrugged it off and didn't think much about it after that.

We were at Grayson's apartment one Saturday morning and his phone was constantly ringing, but he continuously ignored it. All of a sudden, I heard "Boom, boom, boom" on the door; I almost jumped out of my skin and jumped off the bed where we were watching television. Grayson ran to the door, looked through the peephole, and heard him say "shitttttt. The next thing I heard was a chick screaming, "You better open the door; I know you're in there with that African chick." I was confused; I turned to him and asked what the heck was going on. Now, unless his fiancée's ghost was the one banging on the door, he had some explaining to do.

He opened the door, and a chick, who I will call Draya, barged in the door, stood right in front of me, and we both said, "I know you." We attended the same college, and I had seen her in the cafeteria a couple of times. She proceeded to tell me she had been seeing Grayson for a while, pretty much since his son's mother passed away, and she was the one who helped him deal with her loss. I felt like I was in a movie because it was the same stereotypical crap. He stood there and didn't say anything for a while.

Finally, he spoke up and addressed Draya, "You're crazy! I've told you I don't want to be with you and you won't let me be. I'm with her now," pointing to me.

She responded with, "If that's the case, why are you still living in *my* apartment?" She turned to me and said, "I bet he didn't tell you this apartment is in my name and he sells drugs!" I gasped! I couldn't believe all I just heard. I grabbed my things and walked out, leaving both of them in the room.

I was stunned and couldn't believe I had been so stupid by dating the type of person I hadn't wanted to. I got home and was still trying to process what had happened when my doorbell rang. Of course, it was Grayson. He explained that he had been seeing Draya before he met me but it was more of a friends with benefits situation and not a real relationship. He had told her repeatedly he was done, but she wouldn't let him go. He called her while I was there to let her know he was serious about him not wanting to be with her. She begged and hollered, and when she saw it was getting her nowhere, she asked that he move out of his apartment since the apartment was in her name. I asked about the drugs, and he said she was making it up because she was mad at him. He told me the reason he had gotten her to get his apartment in her name is that his credit was messed up.

Grayson then asked me if I would be willing to help him by getting him an apartment in my name, so he could get rid of the crazy girl. Being young and naïve, I didn't think it was that big of a deal to get an apartment in my name, so I agreed. I also put his car in my name (covers face in shame. In my defence though, I made him pay the first three months' rent, a year of car payments as well as had him sign an agreement saying he was going to pay off the car by the following year). He moved into the apartment and about a week later, sat me down, and told me what he really did for a living: yup, he sold drugs. I thought I was in a movie and while I was a bit scared, a part of me actually liked the idea—my real life bad boy. I told him I would stay with him as long as he didn't bring the drugs anywhere near me.

Grayson and I had a tumultuous relationship the entire time and I knew I had bit more than I could chew the first time I saw him with a gun. That was when I knew there was nothing cute about having a "bad boy" as a boyfriend. I told him never to bring a gun to my apartment because it made me uncomfortable. I tried to end the relationship several times, but

I was in too deep, especially since his apartment and car were in my name.

We argued constantly and loudly, especially when I found out he was somewhat still involved with Draya. Most of my neighbours knew our relationship was dysfunctional and would call the cops every time we argued. The cops eventually knew me by name; every time they came out; I always protected Grayson because I didn't want to be seen as the girl who got her boyfriend locked up. The cops always advised me to leave him and move on because I was better than that, but I never took their advice.

Relationship Goes from Bad to Worse
I knew I was in serious trouble the first time the relationship went from verbal to physical abuse. While arguing, I must have said something Grayson didn't like because the next thing I felt was pain shooting through my forehead when he hit me on the face with the butt of his phone. I yelled out in pain and started crying. He started saying it was my fault he did that, and if I had shut up when he asked me to, this would not have happened. He left and I remember looking in the mirror and seeing a big lump on my forehead. I was supposed to meet up with my sisters for lunch but cancelled because I didn't want them to know what had happened.

He came back later with flowers and some clothes he had bought for me—evidently, a typical abuser behaviour. He apologized and said he would never do it again. I guess like most people in an abusive relationship, I wanted to believe him, but I was wrong. A couple of weeks later, we got into another argument, and as I was mouthing off and walking away from him, I felt the tug on my head as my neck snapped back from him yanking my braids.

I had made a pact with myself that if he ever got physical with me again, that would be it because I refused to be anyone's punching bag. I turned around and with all the strength I could muster, pushed him into the wall. He obviously didn't see that coming, as he crashed and broke the wall with his back ((No, i'm not hulk, the wall was dry wall..Lol). I ran out of the apartment and down the stairs. He came down and I asked him to leave, telling him we were done. Now I had to figure out a way to get the apartment and car out of my name. For the next couple of months, Grayson and I still argued a lot because I would have to talk to him or see him about payments. Even though he was making payments on the car and apartment, he played a lot of games, like not paying the rent and car note on time — on purpose.

One time when his rent was past due, I was furious. I was getting upset and tired of his games, so I started blowing up his phone, and he would either hang up on me or send me to voicemail. He finally called me back the next day, saying he was at the apartment and I could come and pick up the payments before he left. I rushed out because I didn't want to have to deal with his games later on. I got to his apartment and knocked on the door. The door opened and, lo and behold, Draya opened the door. I wasn't even fazed; all I cared about was picking up the rent and car payment. She asked what I wanted and I asked, "Is Grayson here?"

It must not have been the reaction she was hoping for because she responded with, "I asked what you're doing here?" She was starting to get under my skin so I responded with, "You do know this is *my* apartment, and if I want to kick you out, I can but I won't because I'm not here for the drama."

She started taking off her earrings, and I thought to myself, *I wonder why she's taking*...Before I could finish the thought in my head, I felt a sharp stinging pain in my face. I stumbled back but caught myself before I fell.

For what seemed like an eternity, I stood there lost, deciding what to do. I had always said if I were ever in a situation like that, I would walk away for two reasons: I had never been in a fight with anyone except my sisters and didn't want to get beat up and I also didn't want people thinking I was fighting over a guy. But at that moment, all the reasons I had given myself to never fight flew out the window. I chose to defend myself because I was sure if I didn't, she would try to bully me every time she saw me in college. I threw a punch, but it didn't really hit her hard. Then I felt her grab my braids and next thing I saw, they were all over the floor. That was when the hulk in me came out. I threw her to the floor, sat on her, and every time I thought of having to *cut gorimapa* (go bald), I punched her. She managed to wiggle herself free, but I got her back down and stomped on her face with my timbs a couple of times. She started screaming for help and that was when Grayson ran out to break her free.

Jail Time

Draya started crying and called the cops. When the cops came, she lied and said I hit her first. I explained to the cops what happened, but they didn't believe that she threw the first punch because she was badly beaten. They put me in handcuffs and led me out to the police car. I couldn't believe this was happening. I asked Grayson to let them know he was the one that asked me to come over to pick up the check, that I hadn't just shown up with the purpose of getting in a fight but he also lied.

The police showed me a picture of Draya's face and told me I was in some serious trouble. Her face was swollen, eyes blood filled with a broken nose. That ride down to the police station was one of the longest rides I've ever taken. I kept declaring my innocence, but the cop didn't believe me.

At the police station, I was booked and put into a holding cell, and that was when certain things dawned on me: 1.) I was really in jail and would now have a record against me. 2.) It was the weekend and I would probably be here till Monday. Luckily for me, or more like as Yahuah is always looking out for me, I didn't have to stay for the weekend. But I was in the holding cell for the longest five hours of my life. All I could do was cry, pray and promise Yahuah if I got out of this situation, I would stay far, far away from Grayson.

Finally, a cop came and said it was time to see the judge. I didn't have any prior arrests, so he released me on my own recognizance, i.e. no bail money needed to be paid to the court, and no bond was posted. I did have to promise in writing to appear in court for all upcoming proceedings since Draya pressed charges against me.

The cop on duty asked if I wanted to use the phone to call someone to pick me up, but I was so embarrassed that I didn't want to call anyone. All I wanted to do was go home, take a shower, and crawl into my bed. At that moment, one of the cops who had usually responded to many of the domestic disputes between Grayson and me walked in and offered to take me home. In the car, he explained this was the type of situation they hoped I would never get into, and this was the reason they always advised that I let go of the relationship. I opened up to the cop and told him one reason I felt stuck was because his car and apartment were in my name. He told me they had several police reports on file from the numerous times they came out and I could stop by the station to get them, take it to the leasing office, and use that to break my lease. While it didn't cure all my problems, it was a start and I was very relieved.

The rest of the weekend was a blur. By the time Monday rolled in, I still wasn't ready to face anybody. I called out sick from work and decided to deal with the apartment issue. I went down to the station to pick up the police reports, took them to the leasing office, and it was a breeze breaking the lease. I was told I had till the end of the month to move out. I was tempted to stay home from college and have a pity-party but instead chose to attend my business law class.

I got to class early and talked to the lecturer since he was an actual top-shot Delaware attorney. I already had a good rapport with him, so he was easy to talk to. I told him I was arrested and charged with third-degree assault. He told me it wouldn't result in a felony but would still be punishable by a maximum of one year in jail and a criminal fine of $1000 if found guilty. Now I was really scared. I asked if he would be willing to represent me and he flat out said no, not because he didn't want to but he knew I couldn't afford him, even if he gave me a discount. What he did offer to do was to present the case to the mediation office to see if they would take it. He also advised that should they accept it; Draya had to agree to the mediation since she was the one that filed charges against me. Now I had to figure out a way to have her agree to mediation.

I got a call from Grayson later on that evening; the leasing office had dropped off a letter confirming the termination of lease by the end of the month, and he wanted to know if I would call the leasing office to let them know I wasn't breaking the lease. All I could think was *why in the world would I do that?* He explained, "If you do that, I will have Draya drop the charges. I said, "You can have her drop the charges regardless, since you know she hit me first and all I did was defend myself." I hung up the phone.

About two days later, my phone rang and it was Draya. I asked what she wanted since she had a no-contact order out on me. She said she was calling for two things: she wanted me to pay her to drop the charges, and she wanted me to call the leasing office to let them know I no longer wanted to break my lease. I hung up. I was livid! Not only did she put me in this predicament, but now she was trying to blackmail me.

I got to college the next day and told my lecturer what happened. He asked that I record the conversations if I were able to. He also told me he had spoken to someone about getting the case to mediation, and they were going to be reaching out to Draya sometime next week to see if she was willing to go through mediation.

I knew there was no way I could record her, but I had a plan up my sleeves. I kept praying she would call me back and fortunately, she did. She again asked me to pay her to drop the charges. I said I wasn't able to do that but this time around, I asked her a question, hoping she'd incriminate herself. When I asked why she punched me, she said Grayson had told her I wasn't going to fight back, so her plan was to punch me no matter how things had gone. She said she also didn't like that he had moved out of the apartment she had gotten him and I had gotten him another one. I said, "Okay" and hung up. This happened a couple more times, and it was just what I had hoped would happen.

The next time she called me, I told her not to call me anymore because I had her on tape trying to extort money from me when she had a no-contact order out on me, as well as her confession of hitting me first. I told her I would see her in court, and she would most likely be convicted of perjury and wasting the court's time in a baloney case. She tried to call my bluff, but I told her I would see her in court and hung up.

Mediation Time

A couple of days later, I heard from my lecturer that Draya had agreed to mediation. *Booyah!* She fell for it—hook, line and sinker. On the D-day, I got to the appointment super early because I was nervous. When it was time, I walked in and saw Draya already seated at the table. I took a seat and put a recorder on the table. The mediator advised that I was unable to tape whatever went on. I told him I was aware of that but that was not what the recorder was there for. Draya looked scared; I guess that was when the possibility of me having her on tape hit her. I was bagging up inside because there was nothing on the recorder, it was simply for the effect and an intimidation tactic in case she tried to lie some more. The mediator started by asking her what happened. This time, she told the truth that she hit me first because Grayson had told her I wasn't a fighter so I wouldn't fight back. Then I got to tell my side of the story. The mediator stated that although she had started the fight, I still put her in the hospital, so I was responsible for half of her hospital bills. I was upset, but I figured if I only had to pay $932 with all charges dropped, that in itself was a blessing so I wrote a check for that amount. We were both advised that once we signed the paperwork, we were agreeing that the mediation was successful. Neither one of us could come back to charge one another in regards to the case. We both signed the paperwork and that was done!

I went to school with a pep in my step the next time I had my business law class, I was so grateful to my lecturer and told him that. He told me it was a pleasure to help out and asked that I stay out of trouble and make sure nothing interfered with my education since I was a great student. I finished that class, and sadly, that was the last time I spoke with him. I was thankful to be moving on from a situation that had created so much turmoil in my life.

Derrick, the Romantic, Intelligent, Sleek "Good Guy"

My experience with Grayson had left a bad taste in my mouth, so much so I chose to be single, at least until I stumbled across Derrick about a year later.

I was browsing blackplanet.com in April of 2004, when I saw Derrick's profile. While he was good looking, it was his eyes that got me and I sent him a message telling him just that. We messaged back and forth, making small talk, but I wasn't interested in taking things further. I logged off and the next time I logged in, I had a message from him saying he would like to get to know me and for me to give him a call. I really wasn't in the frame of mind of meeting new people, so I didn't call. A couple of days later, I got another message from him. I decided what the heck, and called him. He couldn't really talk but promised to call as soon as he was done. He called me back a few hours later, and we hit it off. I found out he was moving to Delaware that day from Philly and since he didn't know anyone, he asked if I would like to go out for dinner the following day. I agreed, and he offered to pick me up.

I met him in the parking lot of my apartment building, and the first thing I thought to myself was, *Dang, He's short {5'7}*. I just knew this wouldn't go anywhere but figured I would get a free meal and good conversation out of it. Dinner was a blast! We talked about everything, and he was funny, easy to talk to, was a gentleman, but most of all, intelligent; I quickly forgot about his height. We were so engrossed in our conversation we didn't realise it was closing time. We continued our conversation in the car on our way back to my apartment and sat in the car for another two hours conversing.

By this time, it was almost 1 a.m. I felt very comfortable with him, so I asked if he wanted to come upstairs to continue our conversation rather than sitting in the car. We got in my apartment and continued our conversation till about 4 a.m. We were both tired and since it was late and he didn't know his way around Delaware, I offered for him to stay. I offered him my bed and chose to sleep on the couch. I did that for a few reasons. First, I didn't want to be stuck in the room just in case he went ape sh#% on me. Secondly, I had planned out my route through the balcony for an easy escape. Third, I could easily reach the front door if needed. He left around 6:30a.m and I thanked him for a wonderful evening.

I went back to bed and woke up around noon, quickly checked my phone hoping he would have called—nothing. I was disappointed but not for long because he called later wanting to hang out again.

Breaking Up and Making Up

We became inseparable after that, but the relationship wasn't everything either of us had thought it was going to be. Derrick was a great guy in so many ways. He loved Yahuah, had a great relationship with his mother, romantic, cooked and took me on trips. He treated me well most of the time, but he had his shortcomings (no pun intended). I was by no way an angel in the relationship either since I added my own insecurities to our drama. While I didn't go into the relationship insecure, I had let the issues we had had in the relationship change me. I didn't trust him and became accusing so we broke up and made up so many times in the five years we were together that we lost count. But when I compared him to Grayson, he was a god. We loved each other, and we were determined to make it work, if it was the last thing we did.

One morning after I had stayed over during one of our 'break up but about to get back together' period, I was tidying up his room when under his bed, staring right back at me, was a black, lacy bra. I knew it wasn't my bra because I wasn't missing any bras, and I didn't have any belongings at his apartment. My first thought was to storm into the bathroom where he was taking a shower and slap the crap out of him, but

I thought that would not help the situation so I composed myself. I was still debating on what to do, when I heard him turn off the shower and he stepped out of the tub. I immediately ran to the bathroom door and as he opened the door, I was standing there with the bra on my finger, and I asked, "What's this? I found it under the bed."

I expected him to start stuttering, but this dude didn't even flinch. He responded, "What do you mean, what's this? It's a bra and it's yours."
I did a double take—did this dude just say the bra is mine? I said, "I know my bras and this is definitely not one of them but let's say it is, why would it be under your bed?"

He said, "I don't know, maybe it rolled under the bed from when we did laundry."   "Laundry?   Laundry?"   I yelled, "I haven't done laundry with you in a while because we've not been together, remember?" Shaggy's song "It Wasn't Me" started playing in my head, and I knew he would never admit to anything. We both knew the truth: a black lacy bra not belonging to me was in his room, meaning another girl had been there. I loved him, so I justified it, technically, we are not together.

Festering Tree
Unbeknownst to me at the time, the festering seed had taken root in us. A festering tree is a result of continuing to live in a condition of decline and there are several ways for a festering tree to take root in a relationship. The seed may get planted

from disagreements that are not dealt with but swept under the rug. Couples may hold things against each other. Sometimes, both parties care more about feeding their pride or ego much more than resolving issues, so both parties are resentful of each other. With every unresolved issue, the seed gets watered, grows into a plant, and eventually becomes a tree (this is often known as irreconcilable differences). Once this happens, the relationship is over; unless of course, both parties make a conscious effort to save the relationship. This is the stage in the relationship where all you can see are the negative fruits of the festering tree.

Derrick and I were definitely experiencing the fruit of the festering tree. I started sneaking around to check his phone and accused him of cheating even, when he wasn't. Despite our many issues, we genuinely loved each other. We remained adamant about making the relationship work, even when we both knew deep down inside we weren't good for each other. There was so much water under the bridge, the festering tree had taken root, and so the relationship was doomed.

Dream Land

In June of 2007, after one of our "just getting back together" moments and moving in together, Derrick proposed. Looking back, it was his way of showing me he was ready to be committed to our relationship but truthfully, I don't believe he was ready to get married even though he thought he was (I know I wasn't even though I siked myself into believing I was).

The night Derrick proposed to me, I had a dream. In the dream, I was about six months pregnant and held onto the hand of a little boy around three to four years old outside of a house, which I presume was our home. My husband had just pulled up in the driveway; so my son and I were standing outside waiting to welcome him home. When he exited the car, I saw he was tall, dark, and handsome with a shaved head. I woke up and wondered what the dream was about because the person I was married to in that dream was clearly not Derrick. I racked my brain to see if I knew who that was but I didn't, so I shrugged it off as nothing more than a trip to la-la land. I didn't share the dream with anyone because I didn't want people telling me it was my doubts about my relationship manifesting through my dreams. I tried to forget it but couldn't. It was one of those dreams that just always stayed with me.

Our wedding was set for July 19, 2008, a date that was also Derrick's birthday. I had recently been given an opportunity at work to either get laid off with a great severance package or get demoted; I opted for the former and began working in Real Estate full time, so life seemed good in most ways, although Derrick and I continued to argue. About five weeks before the wedding, we got into an argument about my decision to hyphenate my last name. He had agreed to this in the past, but suddenly he had a change of heart and we stopped talking for the next two days.

Downward Spiral

One month before the wedding, I guess his festering tree fully blossomed. Derrick came home and told me the wedding was off. I thought he was just tripping! Everything was paid for; all we had to do was walk down the aisle and say, "I do." I thought to myself, *He can't be serious; he just needs some space.* So I called one of my girlfriends to meet me for drinks. By the time I got back, he was asleep on the couch so I called it a night. He didn't talk to me the next morning, but when he came home that evening, he handed me a stack of papers entitled "Cancellation of Engagement." He was serious. I begged, cried, said and did everything under the sun I could to get him to change his mind. Nevertheless, he stuck to his guns about ending the relationship and calling off the wedding.

The events that happened next went really fast and were a blur. By the following weekend, he had moved out. I didn't understand what was happening, my life was collapsing and there was nothing I could do to stop it. *Where do I start to rebuild my life? What would I tell people? What would people say?* I was hurting and there was nothing I could do to make the pain stop. When I became more and more hysterical, the idea of suicide popped in my head, *At least, I won't have to deal with the hurt, the pain, the embarrassment, and the uncertainty of the future.* I went into the medicine cabinet and grabbed the first medicine I found. With tears streaming down my face, I started thinking, *Am I really doing this?* And I was really doing it; I walked to the refrigerator and grabbed a can of beer. I started popping the pills and washing them down with the beer.

At the last minute, I decided to write a suicide note. At least, that would help my family know why I did it (I really thought it would help). As I was writing my suicide note, my cousin Fey called me. I looked at my phone and thought to myself, *why are you calling me? Leave me alone, I just want to die in peace.* Something prompted me to answer the phone. She asked me why I sounded funny and for some reason, I told her what I had done but later said I was joking. She hung up the phone and called my sister. My sister Sade called me and asked what I was doing; by this time, I was already losing consciousness.

What felt like the next minute was Sade busting into my apartment and carrying me out to the car, all the while crying and screaming for help at the top of her lungs. She rushed me to the hospital, and all I could hear as I was losing consciousness was, "Bola, please stay with me; you're going to be okay."

Yahuah had a different plan for me. The doctors revived me at the hospital, and when I came to, my mom and sisters were around my bed with concerned looks on their faces. My mom looked as if she had aged about a hundred years from the last time I saw her. She looked at me with tears streaming down her face. For the first time, I forgot about my own problems and realised what I had just done to my family. I cried and apologised for putting them through this hell. I finally asked if Derrick knew what happened since he wasn't in the hospital. They confirmed he knew but didn't show. It was like a ton of bricks hit me: *I attempted to take my life and he didn't care enough to show up?* It was the confirmation I needed to know it was time for me to move on because Yahuah had something better for me. The crazy thing is, I was that one who judged people who tried to commit or committed suicide. It seemed like such a selfish thing to do, but in my weak moment, I succumbed to the same thing I criticised people for. You never know what people are feeling till you've walked in their shoes.

Moving On

I moved in with my mom after I left the hospital, so she could keep an eye on me. Although I hated how over-protective she'd become, I knew I only had myself to blame. I made a plan to stay with her for about a year, save up some money, and then buy a house. I was depressed and cried every day. I hated how everyone looked at me with pity since I was back in my mama's house after being on my own for seven years. All I wanted was to be happy and for my life to be "normal" again. Life sucked, and I felt I couldn't take it anymore.

Only Yeshua Could Heal Me

One day in late July of 2008, I got sick and tired of being sick and tired. I dropped to my knees, crying, and talking to Yeshua. I asked Him to come into my life to direct me. I was tired of being depressed, and I needed to be happy again. I finally knew the choices I was making were not going to fix me. This was beyond me. Only Yeshua could heal me.

Up to this point, I really hadn't thought too much about Yahuah or needing Yeshua in my life. I had gone to church sometimes, but that was the height of it. I found Yeshua and from this point forward, my life would be different because of my relationship with Him. Relying on Christ, I slowly got my strength back and went back to work as a Real Estate agent.

About a week later, I was showing some of my clients a house, and even though I didn't think much about it at the time, all weekend for some reason, I couldn't stop thinking about that house. On Monday, I drove back out to see the house and it felt like home. I wanted this house, but decided to pray on it since it was not in my plans. I prayed all week and felt in my heart it was the right decision to make, so I asked Yahuah to show me a sign even as I was going to move on with the purchase of the house.

When I got to the office which I shared with my sister Sade, I asked her to represent me in the purchase. She wrote up the offer, I signed it, and as I was about to write her a check for the deposit on the house, she turned to me and asked, "Bola, are you sure you're ready to do this? It's exciting and all, but you also have to take into account that it's also going to be a huge responsibility with the maintenance and so on."

It was as if she had read my mind because that was exactly what I was thinking when I was signing the offer. I figured this was the sign I was waiting on from Yahuah; maybe it wasn't the right time I thought to myself. I was about to say to her, "You know, I'm not so sure, maybe this is an impulse move, I may be in over my head," when my eyes darted to my check book and the check number was 772. I immediately knew this was the sign I was waiting on from Yahuah; Yahuah was telling me this was the home for me because the house number was also 772. I moved ahead with the offer and it was accepted. I moved into my home on September 27, 2008. It was bittersweet because Derrick and I had made plans to buy a house once we were married. Nevertheless, this new start in a new home was exactly what I needed. I was able to focus my attention on something else other than my broken heart.

Two Steps Forward, Two Steps Back
Valentine's Day 2009 was like any other day till I got a text from Derrick saying, "You were cried for today, I miss you. You don't have to respond to this message; I just wanted you to know." I didn't respond because this was his M.O., and I knew exactly what would happen if I responded. Despite my good intentions, my heart took over and two days later, I responded to the text. We started talking every day, then hanging out, and like old times, we fell back into our routine and decided to give it another shot, then he moved in with me.

Once we settled in the relationship, I think we both knew we had made a huge mistake, but we really wanted things to work out so we pretended like everything was okay. We found ourselves walking on eggshells around each other. I couldn't be myself, as I didn't want to say or do the wrong things before he turned around and broke up with me again. We took a trip to

Jamaica in July to try to jumpstart our relationship and even that didn't help. Things didn't quite gel with us, and I found myself counting down the days before we came back home.

Finally, we were back home, but things went from bad to worse. After a huge fight the day we got back, I knew I needed a break. My sisters and I decided on a girls' trip to New York City for the weekend. All the while I was in New York, I found myself dreading going back home to Derrick.

For the first time in my life, I found myself saying a prayer I had never said before about a guy. I asked Yahuah to remove Derrick from my life if he wasn't the one He had ordained for me. I was shocked because before that moment, my prayers had consisted of me praying for Yahuah to make the relationship work. I got home and I can't say we were happy to see each other, but we acted like we were.

The next day, we both worked from home so we could spend some time together. We were having a random conversation when I asked, "If you were not with me, is there someone you would rather be with?" I don't even know where that came from, but I asked it anyway.

He said, "No, but I guess I should let you know now that I've decided not to get married because I don't believe in marriage anymore." I was like, "Huh? We were engaged to be married and now you tell me you don't want to get married?" I was about to go into my usual long rant, but I remembered my prayer so I figured Yahuah was trying to tell me something. I told him it was fine with me, but I knew I was ordained to be someone's wife so maybe it was best to call it quits. He moved out about two weeks later and while I was sad, I knew it was the best thing for us. As time went on, I knew he wasn't the man for me.

Fast forward to October of 2009, the day of the World Series, I got a text from "you know who" saying he had hurt his back and wanted to know if I could keep him company by having dinner with him. I thought to myself, *here we go again*. I responded that I was busy, but he was adamant and I eventually gave in. He gave me his address to pick him up because he couldn't drive and I didn't know where he lived. When I saw him, I realised I still had some feelings for him, but I wasn't in love with him anymore. We made small talk over dinner and drinks, but it all just felt weird. I asked if he was seeing anyone, and he said he was but it was nothing serious. I dropped him back off after dinner and went back home.

As soon as I pulled up to the house, I got a call from him saying I should have come upstairs for a tour of his loft. I was thinking, *really, a tour of your loft or something else?* Anyway, I told him I could tour the loft some other time, but he begged for me to come back. Mind you, this was around 11:30 p.m., but you already know how it ended. I gave in and got in the car but my car wouldn't start. I tried to start it for fifteen minutes straight, nothing. I called Derrick to let him know I wouldn't be able to make it. He asked for me to keep trying and voila, the car started. It was the weirdest thing ever. As I was driving back to him, I saw an accident scene that wasn't there when I drove past the spot less than thirty minutes before (a car had hit a deer). I really believe that accident would have happened to me, but Yahuah was looking out for me even though I was being disobedient.

I got to his loft and I must say it was beautiful. The view was incredible and the lighting was perfect. To say the least, it was romantic, and you guessed it, I "gave up the cookie." This led to me seeing him every day for the next week. I knew I was repeating the same cycle and I didn't want that for myself, so I kept praying and asking for Yahuah to be my guide. I was flipping channels one day and came across a preacher talking about the Ishmael and Isaac theory.

Ishmael and Isaac

There is a story in the Book of Genesis where Yahuah promised Abraham a son who will be birthed by his wife, Sarah. The only problem was, Sarah was barren and as they aged, Sarah became impatient and arranged for a child to be born to Abraham through her own Egyptian maidservant Hagar. Ishmael was born from this arrangement (See Genesis 16:1- 4). While Abraham and Sarah took it upon themselves to "help" Yahuah, Yahuah's plan didn't change. He kept His word and brought the promise to fruition the way He had already told Abraham it would play out.

How can we use this story to understand Yahuah's plan for relationships? Ishmael is the man or woman you take upon yourself to be your husband or wife, instead of the rightful person Yahuah has ordained for you. In the same way Sarah grew impatient, you might choose a spouse based on your own desires—this is your Ishmael. Ishmael may seem to be everything you've ever wanted but unless you have sought Yahuah, this will never be who Yahuah wants for you. On the other hand, when Yahuah directs you, you will end up with your Isaac, the spouse Yahuah wants for you. Let me add, in many cases, he will be the least type of person you would expect and pick for yourself. But when you open yourself up to Yahuah's possibilities, it turns out to be the best thing ever.

I knew Yahuah was telling me Derrick wasn't the one for me, and it was time to move on. But he was familiar, and I didn't want to start all over again, especially after being with him off and on for five years. The following day, Derrick stayed over and when he was getting ready for work the next morning, I started thinking to myself, *this past week I've spent with him has done nothing for me, and nothing has changed. If I don't end this now, I'm going to be playing this game for the rest of my life.* I went upstairs to him with my voice shaking and feeling very uncertain. I told him I was done and I couldn't do this anymore. I told him while I still cared about him, I loved myself more and I was tired and I wanted more out of life and a relationship. We both deserved better.

I asked that when he stepped out of the door, not to contact me anymore, not because I hated him or anything, but for us to be able to stop the cycle. He said, "I wasn't asking for us to get back together; I saw it as us having fun." He said he knew this day would come, but he didn't think it would come this soon. I side-eyed him, and thought, *this soon? Are you kidding me? It took me five years and a failed suicide attempt to get to this decision and you think it's soon?*

The next couple of days were not easy, as the doubt kicked in, and I started asking Yahuah if I had made the right decision. I wanted to call him so badly, but every time I felt the urge, I said a prayer instead.

About a week later, I was listening to Coco Brotha on Praise FM on my drive home from the office. I pulled into my driveway but sat in the car to continue to listen. From nowhere Coco Brotha said, "I want you to know you're Yahuah's daughter and He has someone better in store for you; you made the right decision. Don't let the doubts reel you back in." Then he said, "I don't know where that came from, but I guess Yahuah had to do His work and I pray that blesses someone." I knew that was Yahuah talking to me and I needed to let Derrick go.

The next day, my dad called and asked how I was doing. I told him I was doing well and then he asked about Derrick (it was surprising because my dad hardly ever butted into any of our relationships). I told him I wasn't seeing him anymore and I was DONE.

My dad said, "That's good to know; I usually don't like to butt into your relationships, but I think enough is enough; you went through a lot with Derrick, especially when he called off the wedding. If you go back to him, I'm going to have to make the tough decision of disowning you." *Dang Daddy, it's like that?* I assured him I had moved on from that situation so he had nothing to worry about. That conversation with my dad definitely helped my cause.

Christmas day 2009, while I was getting ready to go to Christmas dinner, my sister Titi called. The first thing she said was, "You will never guess who just got engaged!"

"Who?" I asked.

"Derrick," she said with disgust in her voice. My heart skipped as I had flashbacks of our relationship. I felt an overwhelming peace and joy come over me because I knew our chapter was officially over, I told her I was very happy for him but she didn't believe me, yet I didn't feel I had to convince her because I didn't care. I had closed that chapter of my life just like he had.

Relationships can be challenging, but they shouldn't be as hard as ours had been. I am thankful Derrick had the courage to call off the wedding when he did. If he hadn't done that, we would have had a miserable marriage and missed out on the wonderful people we both ended up with.

All in all, the relationships I've been in have taught me some major life lessons.

Life Lessons Picked Up Along the Way

1.   Love yourself; no one can love you like you and you cannot love anyone or receive love unless you do.

2.   Do NOT look for love. Work on yourself and be the best person you can be in a relationship and love will find you.

3.   Everything that glitters isn't gold. No matter how good someone may look (packaging), pay attention to their actions because many people talk a good game but can't back it up.

4.   We all hear people say he/she has potential. The truth is we ALL have potential, but not all of us live up to our potential. It's better to go with people's fruits and patterns (a person's life resume of decisions and outcomes as well as repeated behaviour), as opposed to what we think they can do/become. This doesn't mean we should write off people who haven't yet come into their own. But before you get involved, ask yourself, "Are they using their potential now? What are their fruits (results of their actions)? What are their patterns (repeated behaviour)? Someone may be packaged right, but if what they have to show for themselves is mostly negative fruits and patterns, chances are this situation will turn out the same way, unless you see them making a conscious effort to do things differently on a daily basis. Never accept just future potential.

5.   No matter how alone you feel, never allow yourself to cross into the realm of loneliness. Loneliness will make you lower your standards and accept things you ordinarily wouldn't. You'll do questionable things, you'll make poor decisions, and you'll end up feeling worse about yourself. You will find yourself dating people on your "do not date list," all because you don't want to be lonely. Stay off social media and the fake reality most people invent for themselves. Back away from loneliness. Yes, you may be single, but use this time to reflect on what it is you want out of life; use your time

productively—travel, pick up a hobby, start a business, read books, go to the movies, etc. There are so many things you can do aside from constantly dreaming about Mr. or Mrs. Right. *Never* settle for the "frame" of a man/woman i.e. any ol' person because you don't want to be alone. It's not worth the loss of your self-esteem. You will learn to appreciate your singlehood once you get attached that you might even find yourself yearning for it at times. Enjoy your singlehood!

6.   Accept people for who they are and not who you expect them to be. If you cannot accept them as they are, then you should not get into a relationship with them. Most people go into relationships with the hope of their partner changing for the better and then hope things will be perfect. The reality is by the time we cross into our twenties; most of us are set in our ways. While we can work to change some things if we make a conscious effort (most of us don't), for the most part, we are who we are. You need to have an honest conversation with yourself whether those things you don't like about a person are things you are willing to accept and live with; that way, if the person never changes, you live with it, and if they do, it's a plus. Don't set yourself up for failure.

7.   Never regret anything in life especially past/failed relationships because at some point, that relationship was exactly what you wanted or needed. Take it for what it was and learn whatever lesson you were meant to learn. If not, you will continue running into that lesson until you learn it.

8.   No matter how much you might love someone, if you are not good together, you need to walk away before you damage each other.

9.   A man will go hard for what they truly want i.e. will make you a priority, if you're not a priority to him, then you are not what he truly wants. Walk away no matter how much you love him. You want a man that loves you and not just a man you love; there's a difference between the two.

10.   Love yourself; no one can love you like you and you cannot love anyone or receive love unless you do.

Disclaimer: If you've gone ahead and married an Ishmael, unfortunately, you have made your choice, so you have to stick with that marriage. Don't get a divorce on my account by saying he/she's your Ishmael. As we all know, Yahuah hates divorce. The good news is, though, even if you married someone Yahuah did not ordain you for, Yahuah can still bless your marriage, like he blessed Ishmael even as he wasn't the promised child and part of Yahuah's plan. Genesis 17: 20 tells us, *"And as for Ishmael, I have heard thee: Behold, I have blessed him, and will make him fruitful, and will multiply him exceedingly; twelve princes shall be beget, and I will make him a great nation."*

Chapter 4

Blast from the Past

Things fall apart so better things can fall together ~ Marilyn Monroe

Abayomi, the Wise, Illustrious, Handsome, Romantic, Mr. Wonderful

Sometime in 2010, I read something on Twitter that struck a chord with me: how much heartbreak do you have to go through before it is considered self-abuse? I had been chasing love and looking for it in all the wrong places since I was fourteen years old. I was tired of the dating scene and dead-end relationships; I knew it was time to do things differently. I prayed and promised Yahuah that the next man I would date and be intimate with would be my husband. I was ready to meet the man Yahuah had ordained me for, so I went on an intimacy fast. (An intimacy fast is a form of worshipping Yahuah by submitting and honouring your body as Yahuah's temple by not defiling it with sexual sin — fornication which is seen as Harlotry in Yahuah's eyes.)

I decided to do this along with praying continually and fasting, that is, abstaining from food (Food fasting is one of my regular spiritual weapon of choice because it puts us in a position to become attentive to Yahuah. It also positions us for whatever breakthrough we are looking for). The Bible tells us that certain situations require prayer and fasting. Matthew 17:21 reads, *"Howbeit this kind goeth not out but by prayer and fasting."* While we can't earn points with Yahuah because He doesn't look at our "works," He does honour our obedience to Him, especially when we make a decision to die to self. Do it and you will be amazed at the results you will get.

One of my friends, David (thanks bro) sent this Soul Mate Prayer to me and I started saying it in conjunction with my fast.

Dear Yahuah, Loving Essence of all there is,
Please fill me with your sacred presence.
I ask for your Love and Guidance and for your blessings
As I explore the deep reaches of my heart.
I ask for your assistance in releasing that which stands in the way of true love.
My heart is pure; my intentions clear.

Please bring to me my most perfect partner.
I seek a partner, who enhances me by his/her very being,
Who brings more love, joy, peace and prosperity to my life,
Who I can love fully and who can fully receive my love,
Who loves honours and cherishes me completely, and always.
May my heart be open and my head be clear.
May my life be ready to welcome True love.
May I be embraced in a circle of your love and uplifted by your grace.
And so it is in Yeshua's name. Amen ~ Unknown

Disclaimer: This prayer worked for me and I know a couple of people it has also worked for, but it's not "magic." The key is having a contrite heart. You can say this prayer till you are blue in the face. But if your heart is not in the right place, it will NOT work. (It was during this period I understood the meaning of the saying, "Yahuah looks at our heart" because less than a week later, I met "the one," even though I didn't know it then).

The One!

I was getting ready to go into the office the morning of November 2, 2010 when, from nowhere, Abayomi Pacheco, my now wonderful husband, popped into my mind. *I wonder what happened to him,* I thought. I had added him on Facebook about a year and a half ago and talked to him once. During that conversation, he told me he had had a huge crush on me when we were in primary school. I had no idea of that because back then, he was like Dennis the Menace (sorry babe) and was always into some mischief, so I avoided him like the plague. I made a mental note to send him a message to check on him, but I never got around to doing that since I was swamped with work.

Later that evening, I got a message beep on my phone; it was a Facebook chat from none other than Abayomi. I thought, *this is freaky; the day I think about this guy, he sends me a message?* I responded and told him I had thought of him that morning and meant to send him a message to check on him, but he didn't buy it. We had been chatting for about five minutes when he asked if I wanted to talk on Skype. I was bored and had some time to kill so I obliged. I logged on to Skype and was pleasantly surprised. I had expected to see the same rough-looking, troublesome kid I had known in primary school, but he was nothing like I remembered him.

He was dark-skinned and handsome, with a beautiful smile. We started talking and I found him to be super-intelligent, funny, mature, cultured but most of all, very calm. It also didn't hurt that he had a British accent. I couldn't believe this was the same troublesome kid from primary school. We talked for close to seven hours and felt as if we had been friends forever. After we finally logged off, I was really excited about finding a new friend and hoped I would get a chance to talk to him again and soon.

The next day, I logged onto Skype hoping he would be logged on but he wasn't. I felt a slight pang of sadness, but that didn't last too long because he soon was logged on and Skyped me. I waited a while to answer the call because I didn't want him to know I had been waiting to talk to him. Like we did the previous night, we talked for hours. During our conversation, he said, "You know you're going to be my wife, right?"

What?!? He said it again and all I did was laugh and asked how he knew that.

He said, "I don't know how to explain it to you, but I feel it in my gut."

I responded with "Yeah, whatever." I had not really thought about him in that light since he lived on another continent, Africa to be exact, and I didn't do long distance. Plus, he wasn't really the type of guy I was used to dating. I didn't take what he said seriously and changed the subject.

We formed a rather fast and close friendship and started talking every day. The more I got to know about him, the more I liked and wanted to know more as he was different from any guy I had dated. Somehow he charmed me and we started a long distance relationship. I made plans to visit him in Nigeria in February of 2011, but my impatience kicked in. I decided to switch my visit from February to December, wanting to make sure this wasn't a waste of my time. I prayed on it and Yahuah laid it on my heart to wait and not visit till February; I was bummed but obedient and waited till February.

The Meeting

We talked every day on the phone and on Skype and while I loved almost everything about him, I was stuck on the fact that he wasn't really my "typical type" but because I'd been seeking

Yahuah, I was being open-minded and before I knew it, it was time to travel to Nigeria. My plane landed in Lagos in February 2011 and I started getting nervous with different *"what if"* thoughts running through my mind. *What if I see him and he is ugly? What if we don't get along? What if there's no chemistry?* I had a million and one questions and I couldn't wait to see him so I could finally breathe easily.

I walked out of the airport with my bags in tow and I saw him standing there with a HUGE smile. *He's handsome*, I thought to myself, *and has some beautiful teeth*! Major points! We hugged for a while, and then he grabbed my bags and led me to the waiting car. The drive to my dad's house was a bit awkward because I suddenly became shy — I still don't understand for the life of me why that happened, anyway, we got to my house and I introduced him to everyone, talked some more, and then he left. Later on down the line, I found out he went home and told his mother he was going to marry me. The crazy thing was that whenever I introduced him to any one, they always called it and said he was my husband. My sister Dotun was one of them but I still didn't see it.

I stayed in Nigeria for seven weeks. During that period, I got to really know Abayomi and the more I knew about him, the more I loved him but there was a "but". I know as we get older we're supposed to have our priorities in order and certain things shouldn't matter, but I begged to differ. While Abayomi was everything and more than I was looking for in a Husband and Life Partner, he wasn't keen on his appearance. He would throw anything on because he really didn't care. It started affecting my feelings for him and because I didn't know how to bring it to his attention, I decided I would end things with him when I got back to America, even though it wasn't what I wanted. I prayed to Yahuah about it and also spoke to my sister Sade about how I was feeling, including my plans of ending things with him. She told me not to make any rash decisions especially because of what the girl at the train station said. *Wow, that girl; I had completely forgotten about her.* I hung up the phone and thought back to the summer of 2010.

The Girl at the Train Station

My phone rang the morning of August 26, it was my friend Tayo calling to let me know she would be in New York City the second week of September. I was elated about seeing her, since she lived in London and we didn't get to see one another often. I could hardly wait for this trip. September 11 finally came and I rolled out of bed not feeling very excited about anything. I was sad, moody, and depressed, but I couldn't figure out why for the life of me. I got on my knees and prayed, asking for Yahuah to reveal Himself to me by showing me a sign He was truly with me. I called Tayo and told her I wasn't going to make it. Naturally she was upset, but I didn't have it in me to make that trip so I crawled back into bed.

About two hours later, my cell phone rang and I almost didn't pick it up because I didn't recognize the number. However, I am so glad I did because it turned out to be my pastor calling to give me a word of encouragement. The strange thing about this was that in the past, the pastor never called my mobile phone, always my home phone. The pastor said Yahuah placed it on his heart to call me to encourage me. Pastor Hare prayed for me, and I got the rejuvenation that I needed. I was pumped because I knew Yahuah was truly with me.

I called Tayo to let her know I was going to make it after all. I checked the train schedule and decided to catch the 5:30 p.m. train. I packed my things and jumped in the shower, but by the time I was ready, I knew I wouldn't be able to catch the 5:30 p.m. train. I decided to catch the next train leaving at 6:19 p.m. but I got to the station at 6:00 p.m., too late to catch the 6:19 p.m. I figured I would go with the flow and get whatever train was available when I got in there instead of stressing and rushing.

As soon as I stepped into the train station, I saw a girl, and the first thought that popped into my head was, *she looks like someone I could be friends with*. I walked to Starbucks to get my favourite drink; white chocolate mocha. As I walked out of the store, I heard the announcement for my train but missed what track the train was leaving from. I started walking towards the train tracks and there she was again, I stood next to her and asked if she knew what track the New York train was leaving from. She responded, "Track 4."

I picked up on an accent, so I asked where she was from. She responded, "Zimbabwe." I told her I was from Nigeria and we started making small talk. She told me her name was Rumbi and when the train pulled up, she asked if I wanted to sit with her since she was also going to NYC. We found a seat and continued talking. About an hour into our conversations, she stopped mid-sentence and said, "I have something to tell you." In my mind, I was wondering what it could be.

She started with, "I have a message for you from Yahuah." She looked at me like she expected me to look at her half-crazy, but I asked her what it was. She told me that as soon as I walked into the train station and she saw my face (I guess this was the same time I saw her and thought to myself, I could be friends with her), Yahuah told her, "That girl is waiting to meet her husband and I want you to let her know because she's been faithful, I will reveal her husband to her very soon, although he won't be what she expects or what she's used to."

I started crying when she told me that because I knew that was Yahuah's way of letting me know He was still with me. The bonus — I would be meeting my husband soon. I asked why she didn't tell me earlier, she explained that she had decided she wasn't even going to say anything to me because she didn't want me to think she was crazy. She continued, stating if I hadn't asked her what track we were supposed to be at, she wouldn't have said anything to me.

I shared how much I needed to hear that message, especially today because I had been feeling down, and if she hadn't said anything, I would have missed hearing that message from Yahuah. It made me realise it's best to be obedient to instructions, especially when Yahuah asks us to do something like share a message with someone. Most of us shrink back because we don't want to appear crazy when we approach the person, but maybe that person is waiting on that message like I was, maybe that message really changes not just their day for the best, but also the course of their lives. We went back to the previous conversation and exchanged numbers, promising to keep in touch, but I haven't heard from her since that day.

After reminiscing about the girl on the train, I went to Yahuah and asked for him to "open" my heart and eyes and show me if Abayomi was truly the one He had ordained me for. I felt Yahuah telling me to be open-minded and communicate how I was feeling to Abayomi. The question was, how would I do that? How was I going to tell him I didn't like the rugged look without hurting his feelings? I couldn't muster up the courage to tell him face to face, so I took the punk way and sent him a text. I let him know I wanted things to work with us, especially since he was everything and more that I wanted, but I knew the way he dressed wasn't something I could live with. He wasn't happy about the text and responded with, "So you choose someone you want to spend the rest of your life with based on how he dresses? Aren't there more important things?" He was hurt and I felt bad about hurting him but at the same time, I was happy I told him how I felt because the days that followed came with the "new and improved" Abayomi. He showed me that he knows how to be "put together" when he puts in the effort; he was just more focused on more important things. But for me, he put in more effort, and can I say that totally helped our relationship. We were just getting into the groove of things, when it was time for me to go back home. We then continued our relationship long distance.

The Proposal

Abayomi and I had been dating for about eight months, but we knew we wanted to be together forever. Abayomi was going to be in Dubai for business, and since it coincided with his birthday, he asked me to fly down to spend his birthday with him. I really wanted to go, but it wasn't in my budget so I told him I couldn't make it. He let me know he wasn't expecting me to pay my way since he was the one asking me to come down; he just wanted to know if I could make it. He bought my ticket, and I got to Dubai on August 1, 2011, a day before his birthday. The next morning, like a great girlfriend, I woke up really early, snuck out of the room to pick up his birthday cake. When I got back into the room, he was up so I gave him his gifts and his cake; we had breakfast and went out for a day of shopping.

Later on that evening, after dinner, we were walking past a jewellery store when the guy in there motioned for us to come in to see some of the things he had. We walked in and he showed us a beautiful engagement ring. I handed Abayomi the ring and asked him to propose to me. We laughed it off and went on our merry way to meet up with some of his friends at their hotel.

We got to the hotel and headed to the reception desk where we were told the hotel offered gondola rides. We decided to do this while waiting for his friends to arrive. It was a starry night and the weather was beautiful. We settled into the gondola and were enjoying the ride when he started telling me how his life had changed for the better since I came into his life. The next thing I know he got on one knee and grabbed my hand. I didn't really understand what was going on and was about to ask if everything was okay when he pulled out the ring.

It was the screams and claps from the other gondolas around us that jolted me back into reality. *Oh my gosh, he is asking me to marry him. Yes, yes, yes!* It was all a daze. When I came to, our gondola driver handed me some gorgeous red roses. That was when I figured out everything that was going on. Abayomi had planned all this! He was not in Dubai for business; we were not meeting up with his friends. This was all part of the plan to propose to me. I was so happy I was marrying this wonderful man!

TIP: Communication is key in a relationship. While this may sound like a cliché, it's the truth. Our relationship improved when I let him know what my issue was, as shallow as it might have been. It gave him an opportunity to fix something minor but major to me. Without communicating, I would have lost out on a wonderful man. This helped our relationship greatly in other areas, too, as it opened the door to being able to talk about other sensitive and serious issues.

Chapter 5

A Dose of Marriage Reality

"Ile oko, ile eko" – Yoruba saying meaning "The marital home is a school."

{This chapter includes some of my personal life-lessons in marriage. We will look at marriage in depth in a later chapter}.

I'd always heard my mom and older people say in Yoruba that "the marital home is a school," but I always dismissed it, chalking it up to be one of those things old people say. Abayomi and I had no doubt we were meant for each other and eight months later, we were married. On our wedding night, I remembered the dream I had had the day my previous fiancé Derrick proposed to me. Yahuah had been showing me

Derrick wasn't the one for me, and he had ordained me for Abayomi. Abayomi had been the one in that dream. I gave a prayer of thanks that He had called off the wedding to Derrick, sparing us both a lifetime of unhappiness.

Abayomi and I had all the right ingredients for the perfect marriage so I was certain we would be humping around the house like rabbits, without all the problems other married people complained about. Marriage was going to be a piece of cake but my, oh my! Was I in for a rude awakening!

Learning to Be a Wife

Like many females, I had been extremely focused on the wedding but hadn't thought much about life after the wedding. I went into marriage as the same person Abayomi had met that first day in November. Instead of focusing on this new chapter of being a wife, I went in as the same independent, outspoken, bigmouthed and sometimes disrespectful Bolanle. I wasn't submissive and neither was I respectful. I said whatever I wanted to say without much thought as I always felt the need to defend my position, a position that was usually focused on, "I'm a 'Feminist' and I fight for equality." I also felt the need to always feed my ego, so it was my way or the highway. But after much unnecessary screaming matches and fights, I am realising that, in order for a marriage to work, Husbands and Wives, especially the wives have "to train our mouths" for marriage (The things we cannot say to our boss we should not say to a spouse because our spouses have higher authority than our bosses). There has to be a Captain that will man this marriage ship, the person that will hold the course and steer the ship the right way based on Yahuah's principles, the person who will protect his vessel with all his being. And I realised for me; that *is* Abayomi–he possesses all those qualities and more so, he is worth submitting to; especially since I've submitted to bosses, managers, supervisor's etc. with less than stellar qualities. If I can submit to people like that, why not my husband? Someone that loves me and goes out of his way to make me happy and comfortable. I'm learning to submit and let him be the Captain of our ship — (albeit slowly) because I love him and want to continue to enjoy this journey called life with him. So, I've made it my lot in life to make him happy and you know what, it helps me too. What I've found is, a *good* pampered man is a rewarder; they can't help but reward their woman in a good way (it's almost as if there's an auto pilot button installed in him, a man gets pampered and boom, he's reciprocating).

Most of us enter into marriage not fully understanding what marriage is truly about (in addition to not knowing the biblical meaning of marriage and the conditions that come with it, I didn't even know what my husband's expectations were). Yes, Abayomi and I had taken the "five languages of love" test based on Gary Chapman's excellent book, *The 5 Love Languages* and had gone to premarital classes. I knew he wanted the basics: respect, support, cooking, cleaning and sex, but, as it would turn out, there's more to a marriage than that. I went into this marriage blind, which is like going into a job knowing what your job description is but not knowing what the company or your boss expects of you. So you put in your time and effort to do whatever you think is best, only to find out your boss isn't happy because there are some things he expects you to do but you didn't do simply because neither of you thought it important enough to verbalise those expectations, you just assumed they know what your expectations are and will make it happen.

We are all different people with different values, beliefs, and expectations. What I may think is important may not be on the same level of importance for you. The saying, "The way to a man's heart is through his stomach," is thrown around a lot, and while there is some truth behind that statement, it's not the be all and end all. I'm pretty sure a man who can cook won't care as much about that as some other issues. What I'm trying to say is this: know thy man! The way to my husband's heart, it turned out, was not food but respect and sex with me! He loves my food, but he loves my body even more. While I was more concerned about making sure his food was cooked and the house was clean, it wasn't that big of a deal to him because he's equally a great cook. As much as we may want them to be, our partners aren't mind readers and neither are we. Before we get into any relationship, especially marriage, we should know each other's expectations. Love waxes and wanes a lot in marriage, and both parties have to make a conscious effort of meeting the other person's needs. Marriage is all about the other person's feelings and interests being met while yours is secondary. But most of us go into marriage thinking about our own happiness and failing miserably at keeping a happy marriage. It is not an easy process and should not be gone into lightly but we jump into it because we love the idea of togetherness but don't want to do the job of staying together. Some of the questions to ask yourself before you decide to get married are: Are you ready to put someone's happiness ahead of yours? Are you ready to LOVE and be with ONE person for the rest of your life forsaking all others, NO MATTER what happens? Are you ready to have their back NO MATTER what happens? Are you ready to have sex with ONLY this person for the rest of your life? Are you ready to wake up to seeing this person's face for the rest of your life? Are you ready to put your life in this person's hands? Are you willing to make this person happy for the rest of your life? Doing things like these is what Author Gary Chapman explains, will keep the "love tank" full.

Chapter 6

Baby Evan

Every child born into the world is a new thought of Yahuah, an
ever-fresh and radiant possibility
~ Kate Douglas Wiggin

Marriage was fun and tough at the same time. Although we bumped heads sometimes, we were happy most of the time. We had found out in November 2013 we were pregnant, so it was a really exciting time of our lives. March 28, 2014 rolled around like any other day. Abayomi was off from work that day, so we were home, hanging out, eating and watching television, when he got a call from work. He got up and went into the kitchen. I couldn't hear the conversation but when he walked out, I could tell something was very wrong because the look of worry and panic were written all over his face. He hung up and told me he had been let go from work. *What?!Are you kidding me? Did I hear that right?* All I wanted to do was break down and ask how we were going to survive since I had been slowing down with work because of the pregnancy. But I knew it wasn't the right time and place for that. I hugged him and told him everything would be all right because Yahuah was in control. We talked about what we could do in the meantime. He started applying for jobs immediately and ended up applying for unemployment the following week.

Job Hunting

Abayomi had been applying for jobs for a while and hadn't heard anything back and was starting to get frustrated so I took over the job application process from him to lessen the burden of applying for jobs. He had also been taking side jobs i.e. painting and landscaping to make sure we didn't starve. He had applied for a job at the company he works at now, for the position he's currently in but hadn't gotten a response yet.

Unknowingly, I had also applied in his name to the same company for a customer service position. It was below his pay grade, but I figured it was a way to get into the company. About a week later, they called him to schedule an interview for the customer service position for the following Monday. Monday came rather quickly, and as he was getting ready for the interview, he mentioned he didn't really feel like going to the interview because it wasn't the position he wanted. I told him,

"Just go, you never know; they may offer you a different and better position." He replied, "When has that ever happened?" I responded, "Favour is not fair; go and see what happens."

He went for the interview and as you may have guessed or not, he was offered a different and better position with more money. It still didn't afford us to do a lot of extracurricular activities but at least, all our bills were paid, and we would be able to take care of our baby. Fast forward about four months later, the company he had gotten let go from filed bankruptcy and shut down. If he hadn't been let go when he was, he would have been out of a job when the company went bankrupt which would have been horrible for us because it was around the same time the baby was due. Thankfully, Yahuah was looking out for us as usual.

Stuck at the Hospital

My pregnancy went smoothly and I loved being pregnant, to the point I prayed to deliver the baby exactly a week late (While I don't believe in astrology, I still didn't want my baby's birth date associated with the word cancer). Two days past my due date, I was still full of energy and working in Real Estate showing homes. A week later, I was still going strong. Nine days overdue, still nothing; Baby Evan wasn't ready to grace us with his presence. That's when I started thinking the person who came up with the saying, "Be careful what you wish for," was on to something. At ten days overdue, I started getting antsy. Even though I was still comfortable, I was ready to hold my baby. My doctor (Dr Frank) and I switched to plan B: the induction plan we had previously talked about. I was scheduled for induction on a Tuesday, but I didn't get a room till Wednesday night around 10 p.m. I went in thinking, *by this time tomorrow, I will be holding my baby*. I had no idea what was coming hence why the Bible tells us in Proverbs 16:9 "*A man's heart plans his way, but Yahuah directs his steps*" (NKJV).

For starters, Dr Frank was not available and would not be available till the following Monday, then I was told I couldn't eat and I was going to be lying in bed for the next twelve hours. The nurse attached a catheter to me and stuck something up my *Vjayjay*. This was supposed to help me contract and open my cervix. Twelve hours later, a little contraction but no open cervix, so they had to repeat the process. That happened one more time and it still didn't work. They changed their course of action and put in something else and I had to stay lying down for another six hours. Six hours later, it hadn't worked, so they doubled the dose, meaning another six hours lying down. I was given ice chips and crackers to help ease my hunger, but it did nothing but made it worse. This process continued for a total of two days.

When all these measures failed, the doctor (Dr Rosalie) decided on Pitocin. When the pain kicked in and became unbearable, I asked for the epidural. As time went on, we were told Evan's heart rate was dropping, so they turned off the

Pitocin to see if my body would dilate by itself; it didn't. It was a very frustrating experience, to say the least.

I had prayed against having a C-Section because I wanted to experience natural delivery with the pushing pains so I could feel like a "real" women. I was determined to get this baby out of me if it was the last thing I did. So I walked around the hospital over and over again. I even got my sisters to walk with me. I danced and did all I knew to do to bring about labour but nothing happened. This went on a total of another two days.

Monday morning, when Dr Frank walked into my room, he was shocked to see I was still pregnant that the first thing he exclaimed was, "You're still pregnant!?" He then said, "I'm taking this baby out now." I didn't even fight it; I no longer cared about being considered less of a woman by having a C-Section. I just wanted to hold my baby. I was tired of being pregnant, I was tired of lying in a hospital bed, I was tired of being hungry, but, most of all, I was TIRED OF HEARING FROM MY DAD. It seemed he called every thirty minutes. The last time I had talked to him, he said, "What's taking so long? Tell the doctor to take the baby out via C.S." I knew he was just concerned about the baby and me, but I didn't want to hear that at the time, so I told him I would talk to him later.

When I hung up the phone, I said to my sisters, "The next time daddy calls, tell him I'm sleeping. He's getting me worried and I don't need that right now." They rolled me into the operating room, with Abayomi by my side, and started working on me; I looked up and noticed there were mirrors on the ceiling, allowing me to see the doctors working on my inside. It freaked me the heck out. I told Dr Frank, so he covered me up properly. I started having thoughts of the doctor making a mistake and me dying leaving Abayomi to care for Evan. I immediately started praying and held on tightly to Abayomi's hand. The next thing I heard were Evan's cries and the doctor saying it was a good thing I didn't push because the umbilical cord was wrapped around his neck.

Wow! All this while I was fighting not to have a C-Section because I wanted to be part of some stupid "club," and the C-Section is what ended up saving Evan from harm. My son came into the world on the wonderful day of July 28th. I held onto him tightly, kissed him, and immediately started declaring Yahuah's Word into his ear. When I was done, they took him from me and gave him to Abayomi to hold. When they wheeled me out of that room, my insides were cold and I could not stop shivering. Even though I had been warned about this, I still didn't expect it. The shivers continued for about two hours and finally stopped, and that was when I was able to relax and enjoy my baby and family.

Home with my Family
Finally, it was time to go home and, frankly, I was ready. I had been in the hospital a total of nine long days, but I wasn't getting discharged till around 6 p.m. Around noon, I started feeling woozy. The nurse checked my blood pressure and while it was slightly higher than normal, it was still in the safe range.

When they checked it when it was time for me to be discharged, it was still in the same range as the last reading, but I didn't feel like myself and started to think it was best to stay in the hospital. I told the attending nurse how I was feeling but they went ahead and discharged me. Dr Rosalie told me to keep her on speed dial if anything happened.

I was so happy to be going home and didn't want to have anything to do with the hospital, so much so, when they asked me for my best contact number, I gave them the home phone number, which we never answered. I got discharged, and Evan and I came home to a fantastic "Happy to have you home; welcome" by Abayomi.

It was good to be home, but it also felt foreign because this was the first time I was home with Evan. I didn't even know where or how to start taking care of him. We stayed downstairs for a bit, and then went upstairs to get ready for bed. A while later, I came downstairs and told Abayomi I was putting Evan to bed and I was also going to bed. I asked for him to check on me often because I still felt "off "and had a debilitating headache. I went to bed and woke up the next morning feeling slightly better. Abayomi left for work (He had used up all his days off while I was in the hospital).

I was downstairs in the living room sorting through a pile of baby clothes my friend Stephanie had given me (thanks a lot girly). I started feeling a loud thumping in my head and realised it was the shrill of my phone setting off the thumping. I quickly answered the phone and it was some nurse saying she was five minutes away and wanted to stop by to check on Evan and me. Hmmmm, negatory! I was sure I had given the hospital the house number because I didn't want to hear from them. I asked her how she got my number, and she said she called Abayomi who gave her my cell phone number. Darn him. I was tired of nurses and wanted to be left alone with my family. But then, I figured *what the heck. She's close by, so why not.* I told her I would be outside waiting.

I had barely opened the door, when this older white lady pulled into the driveway. She had a twinkle in her eye and I let her in to discover she was very nice and easy to talk to. She checked on Evan first, and said everything was fine with him but after taking my blood pressure, she looked at me and then took it again. When the result came up, she looked at me funny. I asked her if everything was okay. She said, "Do you feel fine? I assured her I did. She asked, "Have you had problems with your blood pressure in the past?" I told her I hadn't, but before I left the hospital, it was higher than normal. She took my blood pressure again. Then she said, "I don't want to alarm you, but I'm going to have to call your doctor right now. Your blood pressure is elevated and you should be in the hospital."

While she was on the phone with Dr. Frank, I called Abayomi to let him know what was going on. He said he was on his way home. Dr. Frank wasn't able to see me because he was out of town, but said he would have a doctor ready to see me when I got to the hospital's emergency room. She hung up with him and was going to call the ambulance to take me to the hospital, but I insisted Abayomi was on his way home and he would be taking me to the hospital. I called Abayomi to see how far away he was, and he said he was pulling up to the house. She gave me her contact information and left.

To the Hospital Again

I explained to Abayomi what was going on, and we got in the car with our tiny baby in the back and headed to the hospital. We got to the emergency room around 2 p.m. and thankfully they were expecting me, so I was attended to immediately. When the nurse took my blood pressure, it was at 186/112. Looking at me with "big eyes," the nurse asked if I was okay. I said, "I'm fine except I have a banging headache."

He said, "It's a shock you're not having a stroke right now, but we will give you something for the headache." Another nurse came and immediately started me off on IVs. She told me she couldn't allow Abayomi and Evan (because Evan was a baby) into my room to stay but would let them come in to say good night. We said our good byes and I was wheeled off to get an M.R.I and CT scan.

I did the CT scan first and it was a breeze, so I expected the M.R.I to be the same, but can I say, the M.R.I falls into one of the most horrible things I've ever experienced? Lying still for an hour having to listen to that tormenting noise the machine makes is the worst and what's laughable is the fact that they ask you what song you want to listen to, as if you would be able to hear it over the loud noise the machine makes. I still picked

Marvin Sapp to minister to me through his songs even though I couldn't hear him but it helped invoke Yahuah's presence, as the Bible tells us in Matthew 18:20, *"'For where two or three are gathered together in my name, there am I in the midst of them."* The noise made my headache ten times worse, and I couldn't wait till it was over (I pray I NEVER have to experience that machine ever again and I pray you never have to experience it either in Yeshua's mighty name, Amen).

When I came out of the machine, my head felt like there were thunderclouds rolling around in it. I was wheeled off to ICU and the doctor came and told me they were going to start me on magnesium so that I won't have any seizures. *Wait, what? How?* I didn't understand what was going on. I was supposed to be enjoying my husband and son. Instead here I was again tied to a bed with a catheter attached to me as well as having constant magnesium in my arm for eight hours. I asked if I would be able to go home that night since it was Friday and Abayomi's birthday the next day. He told me not a chance and to expect to be there till Monday. I didn't even know when the tears started flowing. All I wanted was to be home enjoying my family but I couldn't. I kept praying for Yahuah to work His miracle so I could go home. I talked on the phone, read books, watched TV, but the hours were not going by fast enough for me.

Around 8 p.m., I picked up the phone to call Abayomi, but all I could do was stare at the phone because for whatever reason, I didn't remember how to make a call. I didn't think much of it, so I put the phone down. I picked up my book to continue reading, but there was something like a light blocking me from being able to read the words. The nurse came in and when I looked at her, she was blurry. I knew she was there but couldn't see her. I said to her, "I don't know what's happening. I know you're there and I'm looking right at you, but I can't really see you." She said she was going to get the doctor and stepped out of the room. The next thing I knew, I felt my body jerking but I wasn't jerking (very weird experience). I thought, *what in the world is going on here?* And then it hit me: *Holy cow, I'm having a seizure.* I tried screaming for help but it was a useless effort, as nothing came out. And I must have blacked out.

When I came to, I saw the doctor and the nurse standing over me. The doctor asked me several questions to test my awareness. He explained they had been trying to avoid seizures by giving me magnesium, but since this hadn't worked, he would up the dose. I was scared but thanked Yahuah for His protection and kept praying for healing.

The next morning was Abayomi's birthday. I called him really early to let him know where I had hidden his gift. I was sad I couldn't spend his birthday doing something other than being in a hospital room, but I was hopeful I would be going home that day. Unfortunately, the doctor burst my bubble when he said I had to get an EEG but the specialist wouldn't be available till Monday. I was bummed but thankful to be alive and in good spirits.

After getting my EEG on Monday, I learnt my blood pressure was not back to what it was normally, but it was back in the safe range. They discharged me but not before being given medication for epilepsy to avoid seizures and high blood pressure, meaning I had to give up breast-feeding. I was told to use it for thirty days and then come back to see the doctor.

Another Unexpected Situation

Three weeks after leaving the hospital, I was doing better and had gotten into my routine as a mum. Abayomi had gone to work, leaving me home alone with Evan. As I was going downstairs with Evan in my arms, I tripped and we fell down the stairs. I tried to get up but my ribs hurt. I was still thinking how painful that was when I remembered, *Evan was in my arms when I fell.* I looked around and saw him at the foot of the stairs. I picked him up, and he looked like he was saying, "Why did you do that?" He started crying and I started praying, I kept looking over him to make sure he wasn't bleeding. He seemed fine, but I didn't know what to do.

I called Abayomi hysterical; he calmed me down and asked me to take Evan to the hospital to be sure nothing was wrong with him and also said to make sure Evan didn't sleep till we got to the hospital. So here I was, driving to the emergency room, trying to make sure Evan didn't fall asleep by pouring water on his face to keep him up. I got to the nearest emergency room, still in shock and pain, only to be told they normally didn't treat babies there but would see what they could do.

I called his doctor and told her what happened, and she asked me to take him to the main children's hospital in Philadelphia. I kept praying till I got to the hospital. They were really nice and understanding, putting me at ease and telling me this wasn't an anomaly as many mothers accidentally dropped their babies more than they are willing to share; hearing that made me feel so much better.

The doctor came and saw Evan; he told me we would have to wait in the room for five hours to be monitored. I felt there was something wrong with him because he was too calm (anyone who knows Evan knows he's a super active child and seeing him that calm didn't seem right). The doctor assured me he was that calm because he had taken an impact. We left the hospital later that evening with nothing wrong with my baby boy. He had just been in shock from the impact; my super active child was back.

Message from my Dad

My dad called the next day and asked how everything was. I told him things were fine, but I slipped, and said I was tired of being in and out of hospitals. He asked, "What do you mean?" I told him I had gotten out of the hospital about three weeks ago but didn't tell him because I didn't want him to worry. This was when my dad told me everything that had been happening on his end.

He told me that one day during my pregnancy while he was at church, one of the prayer women told him to pray for his children, especially the pregnant one. If not, she would die. Of course, no parent wants to hear that, so he immediately went in praying and fasting mode. The day I went into the hospital to have Evan, my dad had a dream that my sisters, Dotun and Titi, came to tell him I passed away while giving birth. He said the dream was so vivid he woke up crying and screaming "No, not my Bola!", only to find out it was a dream. He was so happy but realised it could very well be a reality. This explained why he kept calling back to back while I was in the hospital, but he didn't want to tell me or anybody else, so he suffered in silence. Wow! I felt so bad, especially since we had dubbed him the worrier without knowing his reason. I hung up the phone with him and prayed over my life and my household.

Note: The scripture in Isaiah 54:17 that says *"No weapon that is formed against thee shall prosper and every tongue that shall rise against thee in judgment thou shalt condemn"* is so real. It doesn't mean the weapon won't form but in spite of it forming, it will not prosper. Your body may succumb to whatever it is but as long as you don't confirm it by accepting it/speaking it out loud, it will not prosper. You will come out winning! I also believe another reason I had an amazing bounce back in my health is because I went into the battle (hospital, so to say) reading *Prayers and Promises for SUPERNATURAL CHILDBIRTH* by Jackie Mize. I suggest you get the book; it will bless your life abundantly.

Chapter 7

Spiritual Warfare

For Yahuah did not give us a spirit of timidity or cowardice or fear; but [He has given us a spirit] of power and of love and of sound judgment and personal discipline [abilities that result in a calm, well balanced mind and self control] ~ 2 Timothy 1:7 (AMP)

A couple of days after my accidental fall down the stairs, my oldest sister (Moroun) and I went to visit a couple of her friends. While we were all talking about me being in and out of the hospital, both of the women said at the same time, "it's spiritual warfare." For those who don't know what that means, Yahuah's Word tells us in Ephesians 6:12, *"For we wrestle not against flesh and blood, but against principalities, against powers, against the rulers of the darkness of this world, against spiritual wickedness in high places."* Spiritual warfare occurs when the evil spirit world comes against you. While I had heard of spiritual warfare, I didn't think it had anything to do with my situations. I prayed and asked for discernment in every area of my life but then just shrugged it off.

Several months later, April 22, 2015, to be exact (the day after the Costco incident, told in a later chapter), the day started like any other day. I didn't have plans to go out, so I was straightening up the house when I saw Evan's diaper bag lying around. I picked it up and was about to put it in its place, when I saw the holy water I had gotten from church peeking out of it. I remember how excited I had been about getting that holy water that day—I had wanted to anoint my household, cars and everything I could lay my hands on but here it was, three weeks later and it was still sitting unused in Evan's diaper bag. I took it out and felt a *very* strong urge to anoint everything I could. I anointed Abayomi, Evan, myself, the house, and the cars. I felt a sense of peace and accomplishment when I finished. Abayomi left for work, and, like usual, only Evan and I were home. I read him his Bible and books and then sat him in his bouncer to watch his ABCs. I knew it was time to start working on this book, but like clockwork, I thought of making Real Estate calls instead so I could make some money and to put the book aside for now. A sermon I had heard a pastor preach about living a focused life popped in my head. He had talked about making sure we keep our main purpose the focus of our life and not let other distractions take over our lives to the point where we end up not doing the things that matter. I made the decision to focus on finishing the book and not worry about money. I was determined to break my addiction of "chasing money" and had come up with ideas to do that.

Evan started crying, so I took him to his room to change him. As soon as I laid him on the changing table, I started hearing several voices in my head talking all at the same time. One voice in particular stood out and was saying, "What if you are really crazy and what you call your reality is something you've dreamt up in your mind? The reality is, you are locked up in a mental institution because you kept saying you wanted to write your book but you never did. You just went around saying, 'I have to write my book' over and over, without doing it. I then "saw" myself in what I presume to be a mental institution, in a strait jacket, all doped up, rocking back and forth reciting, "I need to write my book." I looked at Evan and I heard, "You are losing it; you know this is the part where women end up killing their children." I responded in my thoughts, *Well, I'm not one of those women.* I picked Evan up to take him downstairs, when I heard, "Go to the bathroom, put him in the tub, and turn on the water."

Something snapped in me. I was sure these voices were demonic voices and this was part of the spiritual warfare. I had to fight. I asked myself, *why am I putting up with this? I am Yahuah's child and I have authority over the enemy.* I said aloud, "Get behind me Satan! I rebuke you in the mighty name of Yeshua" and ran downstairs with Evan in my arms. I literally needed to feel the light so I put Evan in his bouncer, opened the front door and stood outside in the sun (still within eyeshot of Evan) and immediately, I felt a sense of peace come over me; after a few minutes, I walked back into the house at peace and strong in my spirit.

Recognizing Spiritual Attack

Some will say this experience was a figment of my imagination, or that I'm just plain cuckoo which is fine with me. I know without a doubt my experience was an attack from the devil. You see, the devil will not bother you while you're living in sin. But if you try to get out and start living right, he goes bonkers. Some also say the greatest trick of the devil is convincing people he doesn't exist. I beg to differ and say the greatest trick of the devil is convincing people there is no such thing as the spiritual world. Why would he care about that? So people will think he can only attack them physically, leaving their spiritual life wide open and enabling the devil to go to town. Often, by the time people realise they're in the midst of spiritual warfare, so much damage has already been done. This is why we need to put on Yahuah's Armour as advised in the following verses. Ephesians 6:10-18 are important verses to read and pray out loud every morning, as they protect and tell us how to fight Satan and spiritual attacks. Ephesians 6:10, 11 tells us, *"Finally, my brethren, be strong in Yahuah, and in the power of his might. Put on the whole armour of Yahuah that ye may be able to stand against the wiles of the devil."* Please read the other verses in this passage to learn how to call on Yahuah to fight against the devil.

Once you're privy to how important the spiritual world is, the devil goes in for the kill and his biggest target is your mind. But can I tell you how awesome Yahuah is. He's already given us protection against the devil. 2 Timothy 1:7 promises, *"For Yahuah did not give us a spirit of timidity or cowardice or fear, but [He has given us a spirit] of power and of love and of sound judgment and personal discipline [abilities that result in a calm, well-balanced mind and self-control"* [AMP]. We can't lack something He has already given us. When I look for proof in the Bible of all the people who served Yahuah or look at present day servants of Yahuah, I see none that lacks a sound mind. This lets me know I'm not a candidate for a mental breakdown. Think about this: out of everything in the world that Yahuah could have given us, including love and power, He also gave us a sound mind. Why? Because He knows the devil will attack our minds, and if we are not prepared, we will fail and fall.

The mental spiritual attack I had is typical of how some people slowly start losing their minds. Once those thoughts/voices jump into our heads, instead of us rebuking and speaking Yahuah's words to combat those voices/thoughts, we jump on the bandwagon; and before we know it, we are in cuckoo land.

Yahuah always prepares us for whatever battle we are about to face. I know it was not happenstance that I noticed the holy water that day. I was able to anoint my household and myself before that episode happened. Also, because I know some of Yahuah's Word, I was able to use it to defeat the devil which by the way I could only do because I had started reading my Bible, believed and understood it for myself. Please, let's start reading the Bible for ourselves and ask that Yahuah open our minds so we can understand it. This is the only way we can apply the principles in our lives without completely relying on what our religious leaders or other people are telling us the good Book says. People see and interpret things differently; what may mean something to you may mean something entirely different to me. This is one of the reasons we have people killing and committing atrocities in the name of Yahuah, Allah and whatever else people may call Him. Someone read something a long time ago, misinterpreted it, fed it to people, and continues to feed it to people. The vicious cycle continues because people would rather rely on what a religious leader says than on what Yahuah says in His Word. When Yeshua died for our sins, the veil separating people from heaven and Yahuah (Spirit) was torn. This means Yeshua (Spirit) is now the High Priest and we now get to go through Him instead of through any religious leaders (man). Yahuah wants to reveal Himself to us, but it starts with us spending time fellowshipping with him in the Word and in prayer.

When I was out in the "world" chasing money and not walking in my purpose, the devil was fine with that. But as soon as he saw that I was 'hipped' to how things work in the spiritual world and had made a commitment to Yahuah to walk in my purpose to write this book, the devil flipped on me because he knows he will lose more souls once people hear/read Yahuah's words. In Isaiah 55:10, Yahuah says, *"For as the rain and the snow come down from heaven, and do not return there without watering the earth and making it bear and sprout, and furnishing seed to the sower and bread to the eater; so will My word be which goes forth from My mouth; it will not return to Me empty, without accomplishing what I desire, and without succeeding in the matter for which I sent it"* (NASB). The words spoken by Yahuah for me to share with the world through this book will not return to Yahuah without fulfilling His desires of changing people's lives for the better. In Yeshua's name I pray. Amen.

***

In the following chapters, we'll dig in and find out more about Yahuah. We'll also explore some of the things Yahuah has asked us to avoid so we may live a better life. This section of the book is where I suggest you have your heart open so you may receive what the Holy Spirit has to say to you and by the time you finish reading this book, you will have a greater understanding of Yahuah and your mind renewed (Romans 12:2) in Yeshua's name. Amen.

PART 2

My Beliefs as Derived from the Word

Chapter 8

Creation Story

Then Yahuah said, Let us make man in our image, after our likeness: and let them have dominion over the fish of the sea, and over the fowl of the air, and over the cattle, and over all the earth, and over every creeping thing that creepeth upon the earth. So Yahuah created man in his own image, in the image of Yahuah created he him; male and female, he created them (Genesis 1: 26, 27).

Disclaimer! This is my own account of how things played out in the beginning.

I n order for us to know why and what we were put on this earth for, it is important to know where we came from, and to understand that, we have to understand what Adam lost {see Genesis 3:1-24} and what Yeshua came to restore. So let's go back to the beginning of time.

A long time ago, **YAHUAH**, the King of Heaven and the spirit world looked around heaven and said, "I have so many mansions and not enough people to live in them." At that moment, His eyes gazed upon the earth and He thought, "I have more than enough resources on earth, so why not make and put humans there. He said "I will create a "little" heaven on earth; colonize it and give them a taste of what is up here; that way, they can make the choice of coming to live up here with Us". (Us? Yes, Us." {See John 4:24} *"Yahuah is spirit"* and has more than one Spirit. There's Yahuah, the Father; Yahuah, the Son Yeshua; and Yahuah, the Holy Spirit, also called the Counsellor. These three spirits of Yahuah are referred to as the Trinity). As Yahuah was having that conversation, Satan, known as Lucifer back then, was eavesdropping on the conversation and got extremely happy. Why? Ezekiel 28:13 tells us something about Lucifer, *"You were in Eden, Yahuah's Garden. Every precious stone was your covering: The ruby, the topaz, and the diamond; the beryl, the onyx, and the jasper; the lapis lazuli, the turquoise, and the emerald; and the gold, the workmanship of your settings [timbrels] and sockets [flutes] was in you on the day that you were created they were prepared"* (NASB, emphasis mine). In Hebrew, the word for "settings" is *toph*, which means timbrel, a musical instrument. Likewise, the Hebrew word for "sockets" is *neqeb* and means "pipes, grove, hole." Lucifer probably worshipped before Yahuah and because of Lucifer's exceeding beauty and greatness, some suspect he became prideful. Ezekiel 28:17 continues, *"Your heart was lifted up because of your beauty; you corrupted your wisdom for the sake of your splendour"* (NKJV). (Culled *from Was Lucifer originally an Angel of Worship* by Matt Slick). For more in-depth read on this topic, go to **http://www.allaboutgod.com/story-of-lucifer.htm**.

Lucifer was ecstatic people would be moving to heaven, for he would be able to show off his musical skills, as well as his perfectly orchestrated choir. Because of his growing pride, he was getting tired of performing for Yahuah and the angels. He needed a new audience, so this was music to his ears but he got extremely furious when he heard Yahuah say the people wouldn't be moving into heaven immediately. Without much thought, he jumped out of his hiding place and said, "I think you're going about this all wrong. I think you should bring the people in immediately." (He didn't care that he had been eavesdropping and wasn't supposed to be privy to the information in the first place).

Yahuah cautioned him, "Whoaaaa, I know I've given you some reins over the music department, but that's all you get; you don't get a right to speak on issues that are beyond that. Besides, I can't force people to live up here; they have to want to live up here."

"That's where you are wrong," Satan responded {this very moment where Lucifer rebelled is the moment he turned to Satan}, "You are the King and you can command them to live up here, even if they don't want to. I wish I were king; I would do a better job than you're doing." (This is where Yahuah and Satan differ; Yahuah gives you choice, while Satan forces you to do something even if you don't want to).

Yahuah had had enough of Satan and his huge pride and ego; He had given him numerous chances to do better but he refused to repent. So Yahuah banished him from heaven but before he left, Satan grabbed a bullhorn and made an announcement, "I am leaving this safe heaven. Who is ready to turn up and ditch these goody two shoes and be bad with me? Some angels chose to follow him and those angels are now known as demons. Revelations 12:9 tells us, *"And the great dragon was cast out, that old serpent called the Devil, and Satan, which deceiveth the whole world: he was cast out into the earth, and his angels were cast out with him."* Satan and his demons moved to earth. Once on earth, the devil vowed to destroy Yahuah and everything He created, which is where we come in.

Because we were created by Yahuah, we are Satan's targets. Satan knows without a doubt he has no chance in winning against Yahuah, but he won't go down without a fight. He's in cahoots with the other evil gods and demons in the spirit world, hoping they will have enough power to defeat Yahuah. They, however, are at a disadvantage because light always drowns out the darkness but even with that knowledge,

Satan and his minions haven't stopped tempting and influencing mankind since the beginning of time.

After the drama with the devil, Yahuah started on His project: To create a world on earth for His people to live in. Yahuah created the earth for the arrival of man, using the law of faith and the Holy Spirit to speak things into existence. On one of those days, Yahuah picked a beautiful spot on earth and prepared a beautiful Garden for the first man to live in. Yahuah made the first man in His image, a spirit, but because the creation {man} was going to be living on earth, he needed to have a casing to cover the spirit, so Yahuah used dust to create a house {or body} to cover up the spirit. In other words, man is a spirit with a physical body. Yahuah named the man Adam and gave him dominion {exclusive control} over everything on earth, He put him in the Garden He had prepared for him and named the garden "Eden." Eden was a paradise and had everything in it. Yahuah told Adam he could eat of everything in the Garden **except** the tree of the knowledge of good and evil because the day he does, he will die. Adam wasn't too concerned about eating the fruit because he had noticed something that made him unhappy. Every animal he was going to be taking care of had a mate and he didn't have one. Having noticed Adam's thought, Yahuah put him in a deep sleep during which He removed a rib from Adam and used it to form a partner.

When Adam woke up and saw the woman, he immediately ran to her, grabbed her, and twirled her around. He named her Eve and started professing his love to her. He said, "I will provide for you all of your days." She responded, "I will be your 'help meet' and cater to you all of your days. When you go out to take care of the land and animals, I will be right here waiting till you come home to me. I will take care of Eden and have it as an oasis so when you get home you can rest in my bosom and tell me all about your day and I can help you relax." Adam said, "I will love you all of my days." Eve responded, "And I shall respect and obey your leadership all of my days." Adam was about to say something else when Yahuah cut in by clearing His throat and said, "I see you've met each other." They were standing there, holding each other and looking at each other lovingly. Yahuah said, "I guess we are having the wedding now, those promises you said to each other are part of the marriage terms you are required to commit to if you want to be together. He explained that marriage is a covenant—one which cannot be broken—and asked that they be absolutely certain about going into marriage because no matter what happened, they were stuck together forever, and forever is a long time. Adam and Eve stated their agreement in unison, and Yahuah declared them husband and wife.

As a wedding gift, Yahuah blessed them with the gift of reproduction to bear children (this is a gift that comes automatically with marriage and is bestowed upon ALL marriages that are acceptable in Yahuah's sight. As long as your marriage is between a man and a woman, you WILL be blessed with children. So no matter what the doctors of the world have said, if you haven't received your gift yet, stay in faith and know that it will happen sooner rather than later. If you believe, you shall conceive). He told Eve that she would bring forth children and be responsible for taking care of her husband and children. Yahuah left to allow Adam enjoy his new wife; and enjoy her he did and vice versa.

The next morning, Yahuah went to the Garden to visit with Adam and Eve. They were extremely happy and Yahuah told them why He made them: He colonized the earth by bringing a "little heaven to earth." They said they were on board and were eager to live in "a little heaven on earth." Yahuah said, "I must tell you children that 'actions speak louder than words.' Many people say they want something, but what I've found is that they really don't because they do the opposite of what they say they want. Do you know why? It's the war between the spirit and the flesh."

Yahuah then added, saying, "You have a spirit in you that is in My image; this part of you is always good. But you also have a casing, the physical body. The devil has vowed to destroy everything I create. Because he's cunning, crafty and creative, he has found ways to get to your body {flesh}, so you have to take a stand and not give in to his antics."

***

The ever-sneaky devil was lurking around and saw everything that happened with Yahuah, Adam, and Eve. Yahuah left and Adam also departed to go to work. As soon as Satan saw that Eve was alone, he went to her and the rest we know is history. She ate of the tree and not only did she eat of the tree, she also gave some to her husband. Once they ate of the tree, they realised they were naked — something that was irrelevant to them prior to eating of the tree. They became self-conscious and hid behind trees so that when Yahuah came for His usual daily visit, He wouldn't see their nakedness.

When Yahuah came the next day, they were still hiding and Yahuah asked, "Why are you hiding?" Yahuah already knew what they had done, but He wanted them to tell Him themselves. They said they were naked. Yahuah asked, "How did you know you are naked? Did you eat off of the tree I asked you not to eat of?"

Adam immediately threw Eve under the bus as told in Genesis 3:12, "*And the man said, the woman whom thou gavest to be with me, she gave me of the tree, and I did eat.*" Yahuah became sad, not for His sake but for their sakes, for He knew what their fate would be. They and every human would now be under the curse (by eating of the tree, Adam gave/lost his authority on earth to the devil); they will experience pain and eventually die. Yahuah asked again, "Why did you eat it? I warned you about this."

Adam began to put the blame on Yahuah, and said, "You are Yahuah and you know everything, so you knew we were going to eat of the tree," why put it there in the first place?" Yahuah responded, "Choice. I had to give you a choice. As much as I would like to impose My plan on you, I cannot do that. I have to be fair to you and give you the freedom of choice and that can only be done if you are put in a position to choose. The fact you ate of the tree means you did what you desired. Shielding you from that and not putting the tree in the Garden in order to prevent you from eating of it would have been me imposing MY will on you. You chose to eat of the tree,' so now you will experience the consequences, which is you and your offsprings will know evil, experience pain, and start to die and I also have to banish you from the Garden."

Adam and Eve begged and pleaded to stay in Eden but as much as Yahuah wanted to allow them to, He couldn't. They were tainted and He, Yahuah the Light, cannot co-exist with anything dark. So, Yahuah banished Adam and Eve into the earth outside the Garden of Eden and placed an angel as well as a flaming sword that flashed back and forth to guard the way to the tree of life in case they decided to come back to eat of that tree - which would make them immortal. Yahuah was highly disappointed with Adam but sad because He missed His friends, and although He couldn't walk side by side with them anymore, He still checked on them every day and protected them.

As mankind multiplied, so did the evil on earth. Some people, however, went back to Yahuah's ways—people like Enoch, Noah, Abraham, Joseph, Mary, Deborah, Esther, Ruth, King David, Daniel to name a few. They all made Yahuah proud; but still, evil kept growing. Yahuah then decided it was time to reverse the effects of Adam's sin because He hated to see us suffer and this is where Yeshua comes in.

Everything that has happened on earth goes back to the fall of man when Adam and Eve ate of the forbidden tree. Adam failed at his purpose, but Yahuah's plan for mankind to live in harmony with Yahuah and the heavenly beings didn't fail; the plan is still in motion. There are only two parts to this story: the good and the bad, or the holy and the evil, however you want to refer to them. The devil thought he won when he got Adam and Eve to eat of the tree. However, he didn't know Yahuah had a plan to come to earth in the form of a physical person to defeat him and redeem mankind from his clutches. Satan's reign on earth is almost over because Yeshua is about to come back to defeat him *again* (He's the only one that can); He first defeated him in Round One at Golgotha (the cross). The Bible tells us in John 3:16, "*For this is how God loved the world: He gave his one and only son, so that everyone who believes in him will not perish but have eternal life*" (NLT). This reason is why Yeshua transcends all religions; He's gained victory over the devil to restore something Adam lost that is important to all mankind.

Some people say Yahuah sends people to hell but He doesn't, people make that choice themselves. Hell was created for Satan and his demons and not for mankind. Yahuah laid out principles for mankind that if adhered to would help us live life more abundantly and make our lives easier but we would rather do all the things we know aren't good for us. So, our choices will determine whether we will spend eternity in the New Jerusalem with Yahuah and the citizens of heaven or in the lake of fire and brimstone.

Chapter 9

Purpose

The two most important days in your life are the day you are born and the day you figure out why ~ Mark Twain

Philosopher and Jesuit priest, Pierre Teilhard de Chardin, said, "We are not human beings having a spiritual experience. We are spiritual beings having a human experience." We need to start to understand these important principles:

• We are all spiritual beings and are all connected regardless of our differences.

• Every spirit being (human) has Yahuah's nature and moral character. We may not act like it most of the time, but we possess the genetics

• Yahuah loves order—Heaven is an orderly place—everything works in order as evidenced when we look at how nature works. When we step outside of Yahuah's order, we are no longer in line with Him

• Everything Yahuah created has a purpose, whether we know what that purpose is or not.

Like the Great Dr. Myles Munroe stated in his book, *Understanding the Purpose and Power of Woman*, "The source of so many of our problems in this world lies in the fact that we have lost our sense of purpose and the understanding of what it means to be human as Yahuah created us. The following seven principles of purpose will help us understand Yahuah's original intent for us in creation.

1. Yahuah is full of purpose.

2. Yahuah created everything with a purpose.

3. Not every purpose is known to us, because we have lost our understanding of Yahuah's original intent for us.

4. Where purpose is not known, abuse is inevitable.

5. To discover the purpose of something, never ask the creation (man); ask the Creator (Yahuah).

6. We find our purpose only in the mind of our Maker, Yahuah.

7. Yahuah's purpose is the key to our fulfilment."

I am only going to touch on the most relevant principles Dr. Munroe spoke about. For more in-depth study, I recommend you pick up *Understanding the Purpose and Power of Man* or *Understanding the Purpose and Power of Woman,* as they are truly great books. Dr. Munroe continues to explore the idea of purpose: "Yahuah is full of purpose. He never created anything hoping that it would turn out to be something viable. Yahuah first decided what it was to be, and then He made it. This means Yahuah always begins with a finished product in mind. Now consider these questions: why are humans different from animals? Why is a bird different from a fish? Why are women different from men?"

Dr. Munroe answered these questions with a statement: "Everything is the way it is because of why it was created i.e. because of its purpose. The why dictates the design. Yahuah created everything with the ability to fulfil its purpose. Yahuah's purposes were already planned out ahead of time; everything was already 'made' in the mind of the Maker before He created it. What this means is that Yahuah never gives a purpose to something *after* He has made it; rather, He builds everything to fulfil the specific purpose He already had in mind for it. Yahuah designed everything to function in its purpose, and everything is the way it is because its purpose requires it to be so.

"The purpose of a thing determines its nature, design and features. 1 Corinthians 15:38 affirms this principle, *"But Yahuah gives it [a seed] a body as He pleases, and to each seed its own body"* (NKJV). The passage goes on to say in 1 Corinthians 15:40-41, *"There are also celestial bodies and terrestrial bodies; but the glory of the celestial is one, and the glory of the terrestrial is another. There is one glory of the sun, another glory of the moon, and another glory of the stars; for one star differs from another star in glory"* (NKJV). The sun is meant to do a job that the moon isn't supposed to do, so Yahuah created the moon different from the sun. The moon is made to do its job and no other job. The moon does not give light; it reflects. Therefore, Yahuah did not put any light on the moon. Yahuah also made stars of different sizes and luminosity, for His own purposes. The point is that Yahuah made everything the way it is because of what its purpose is."

Are you starting to get excited? The day I read that, something came alive in me! I had always questioned if I was good enough to carry out my purpose. Then it dawned on me that if Yahuah put it on my heart, it meant He had already empowered me with EVERYTHING I needed to be GREAT at the assignment He put me on this earth for.

We always hear people say, "I don't know my purpose," but I beg to differ because I believe we all do. Yahuah has already told each and every one of us our purpose; we may just choose to not accept or pursue the purpose. Yahuah put each one of us on this earth to make this world a better place by using the "gift" He has placed in us, loving people, sharing the good news of Yeshua's redemption to everyone we meet, and by doing that, we are living out our purpose.

Two Ways to Know Yahuah's Purpose for Your Life

1) If you have an obvious gift — this is the easy one because it's evident to you and anyone that comes in contact with it. Pursue this gift and see where it takes you.

2) If you get an idea that's soooooo foreign to you and you can't seem to shake it off no matter how hard you try; you then slowly start warming up to the idea, maybe even start to think how cool it would be to do it (no matter how scared or nervous it makes you). **This is your purpose** or at least the path to it. Don't delay. Go for it!

DO NOT DIE WITHOUT USING YOUR GIFTS!

Chapter 10

Love

But Yahuah demonstrates his own love for us in this: While we were still sinners, Christ died for us ~ Romans 5: 8

Yahuah showed His love for us by sending His Son to die for us, even after all the sins we've committed against Him. Take a minute to think about that. How many people will do that for people who don't acknowledge them, or do pretty much everything they've instructed them not to do for their own good? I doubt anyone would do that; take for instance someone asking you to die for a "bad" child, one that's constantly terrorising your life and is in and out of trouble. I know I wouldn't do it but Yahuah did, He sent Yeshua to die for our sins.

How Does Yahuah Want Us To Carry Out His Mandate?

The same love Yahuah showed when Yeshua died on the cross for us is the same way He wants us to treat each and every person we come across during our lifetime—a challenging task, I know. John 13:34-35 says, *"A new commandment I give unto you, that ye love one another; as I have loved you, that ye also love one another. By this shall all men know that ye are my disciples, if ye love one to another."* The way Yahuah wants the world to know we are His followers is by loving one another—not by going to church, mosque, synagogue, temple, etc. or by being a church worker or even a Pastor, Imam, or Rabbi. It's by loving one another.

Yahuah wanted us to know about the way to live in love, so He plastered it all over our Torahs, Qurans, and Bibles, yet somehow we conveniently skip those passages. Yahuah went on to give us even more concise ways to love so there would be no questions asked and you know what? These guidelines are great as they cover just about any scenario we may encounter. Don't believe me? Read it for yourself. I'm speaking of what is written in 1 Corinthians 13:1-8. Most of us have heard these verses, but we usually associate it with weddings and reserve it for that. (Abayomi and I even used it when we got married) when this scripture is really for use in our everyday lives.

In a well-known passage of Scripture, 1 Corinthians 13: 1-8, Yahuah gives us guidelines for acting in love. This shows us how to act in pretty much every situation we may find ourselves in: *"Though I speak with the tongues of men and angels, but have not love, I have become sounding brass or a clanging cymbal. And though I have the gift of prophecy, and understand all mysteries and all knowledge, and though I have all faith, so that I could remove mountains, but have not love, I am nothing. And though I bestow all my goods to feed the poor, and though I give my body to be burned, but have not love, it profits me nothing. Love suffers long and is kind; love does not envy; love does not parade itself, is not puffed up, does not behave rudely, does not seek its own, is not provoked, thinks no evil, does not rejoice in iniquity, but rejoices in the truth; bears all things, believes all things, hopes all things, endures all things. Love never fails. But whether there are prophecies, they will fail; whether there are tongues, they will cease; whether there is knowledge, it will vanish away"* (NKJV).

We see here the Bible tells us that we may speak different languages even the language of heaven, hear from God, be wise, have the most faith in the world, be a philanthropist, help the poor, feed the homeless, be an organ donor, donate blood, be a surrogate, be a martyr, etc. but if we don't have LOVE, we are nothing but clanging noise. If every one of us made a decision to practice the type of love laid out above every single day, the world would be a better place. Yahuah wants us to work together in spite of our differences and use love as a guide.

Ants

What do ants have to do with Yahuah? Aside from the fact that Yahuah created them and they are some brilliant insects, nothing much but stay with me; I'm on to something. The other day I was in my yard, about to start a writing session and like every other writing session, I asked the Holy Spirit to direct me. I knew Yahuah wanted me to write about living in love with everyone, especially with the people who are different from us but I had no idea how to write it.

I sat down at my writing space and my eyes landed on some ants moving along the fence, and I noticed something interesting about them. They stopped "to say hi and embrace." Now in actuality, that may not have been what they were doing—they might have just been working and passing things off to each other—but this is what it looked like to me so we are going to stick with that thought. They said "hi" and embraced with almost every ant they came in contact with. I saw it as this: even in their busy day, they still had time to share pleasantries with each other, even if for a second and then it was back to their grind. That process repeated over and over, nonstop. I was in awe and I felt the Holy Spirit saying, "This is how it should be with mankind—loving each other and sharing love with everyone they meet." The next time you see ants, pay attention to their actions and maybe you'll see the hope I have for humanity. I mean, if ants can do it, can't we?

PS: I suggest we all make it a habit of reading 1 Corinthians 13:1-13 frequently (every morning if possible) so we can keep the love "commandments" fresh in our minds as well as use them as a guide when we interact with different people throughout our day.

Chapter 11

Religion

If any man among you seems to be religious, and bridleth not his tongue, but deceiveth his own heart, this man's religion is vain. Pure religion and undefiled before Yahuah and the Father is this, to visit the fatherless and widows in their affliction, and to keep himself unspotted from the world.
~ James 1: 26-27 (KJV)

There's been a lot of talk lately about people losing their religion, which can be a good thing if you are shedding the worldly religion. Religion as the Bible explains in James 1:27 is *"to visit orphans and widows in their trouble, and to keep oneself unspotted from the world"* (NKJV), or as translated in the NCV Bible, *"Religion that Yahuah accepts as pure and without fault is this: caring for orphans or widows who need help, and keeping yourself free from the world's evil influence."* This religion, you don't want to shed. Religion according to the world, on the other hand, is described as "an organized system of beliefs, ceremonies, and rules used to worship a god or a group of gods" (Merriam- Webster Dictionary), or simply, to put belief in a particular system of faith and worship. This religion, you can shed.

Before Christ came into the world, the *term* Christianity did not exist. Acts 11:26 tells us when the term came into existence: "And the disciples were called Christians first in Antioch." I've also read that being called Christians at that time was a derogatory term. But the disciples rocked the name because they were in love with Yeshua and wore the name as a badge of honour.

Monotheistic Religions

Monotheistic religions are religions that believe there is only one Supreme Being. Those religions are Judaism, Christianity and Islam. I've included a comparison chart I found on Wikipedia.

Comparison of Religious Beliefs

	Islam {main page}	Judaism {main page}	Christianity {main page}
Type of theism	strict monotheism	strict monotheism	Trinitarian monotheism
Ultimate reality	one Supreme Being	one Supreme Being	one Supreme Being
Names of Yahuah	Allah {Arabic for Yahuah}	Yahweh, Elohim	Yahweh, the Holy Trinity
	Islamic beliefs about Yahuah	**Jewish beliefs about Yahuah**	**Christian beliefs about Yahuah**
Other spiritual beings	angels, demons, jinn	angels and demons	angels and demons
Revered humans	prophets, imams {especially in Shia}	Prophets	saints, church fathers
	Islamic beliefs	**Jewish beliefs about human**	**Christian beliefs**

	about human nature	nature	about human nature
Identity of Yeshua	true prophet of Yahuah, whose message has been corrupted	false prophet	Son of Yahuah, Yahuah incarnate, saviour of the world
Birth of Yeshua	virgin birth	normal birth	virgin birth
Death of Yeshua	did not die, but ascended into heaven during crucifixion	death by crucifixion	death by crucifixion
Resurrection of Yeshua	Denied	Denied	Affirmed
Second Coming of Yeshua	affirmed	Denied	Affirmed
Divine revelation	through Muhammad, recorded in	through Prophets, recorded in	through Prophets and Yeshua {as

	Qur'an	Bible	Yahuah Himself}, recorded in Bible
View of sacred text	inspired, literal word of Yahuah, inerrant in original languages	views vary	inspired, some believe inerrant in original languages
Human nature	equal ability to do good or evil	two equal impulses, one good and one bad	"original sin" inherited from Adam - tendency towards evil
Means of salvation	correct belief, good deeds, Five Pillars	belief in Yahuah, good deeds	correct belief, faith, good deeds, sacraments {some Protestants emphasize faith alone}
Yahuah's	predestination	divine	predestination,

role in salvation		revelation and forgiveness	various forms of grace
Good afterlife	eternal paradise	views vary: either heaven or no afterlife	eternal heaven
Bad afterlife	eternal hell	views vary: either eternal Gehenna, reincarnation, or no afterlife	eternal hell, temporary purgatory {Catholicism}
	Afterlife in Islam	**Afterlife in Judaism**	**Afterlife in Christianity**
View of fellow Abrahamic religions	Jews and Christians are respected as "People of the Book," but they have wrong beliefs and only partial revelation.	Islam and Christianity are false interpretations and extensions of Judaism.	Judaism is a true religion, but with incomplete revelation. Islam is a false religion.

My belief is that all three monotheistic religions, Judaism, Islam and Christianity, came into existence from the same source—Yahuah. While I may be wrong about the origination of these religions, we can't negate the many similarities they share. In regards to the extreme differences between Islam and the other two religions, I believe the practice of world religion—people relying on their "teachers" to read the Bible, Torah, Quran, etc. and then sharing the message with them. A "teacher's" wrong interpretations coupled with the receiver's interpretations, cultures, values, beliefs are the factors that have caused the stark differences. We see the same thing at work in Christianity and how it's practiced by different denominations. These wrong interpretations are passed on from generation to generation, while the truth lies dormant in the pages of the Book; if only we would read them for ourselves and find out what it really says.

All religions have been tainted and have resorted to promoting their own agendas instead of what they were originally intended to do. I mean, think about it. All three monotheistic religions believe there is only one Supreme Being and He is GOOD. Instead of fighting each other trying to prove what religion is right, we need to focus on our similarities rather than our differences because we are on the same side (good side). We need to treat one another the way we have been instructed by the Most High to do—love one another!

Till we come to understand that we (regardless of what religion we practice) have ALL been called together as Yahuah's children (through Yeshua's death and the Holy Spirits help) to advance His Kingdom and defeat the enemy; Satan. If we continue to focus on our differences, we will continue to bump heads and not be able to move on to fulfilling our purpose of advancing Yahuah's Kingdom. Satan's agenda is for us to misdirect our focus to trivial things like which religion is the real deal. It's time for us to reel it in and focus on what's important, which is sharing the Good News and advancing Yahuah's Kingdom by loving people.

Yeshua did not come to earth to promote a religion. He tells us in Luke 19:10, *"The son of man came to find lost people and save them"* (NCV). Yeshua commanded the disciples to spread the Good News to all the nations of the world. We have to remember Satan's agenda: to steal, kill and destroy. What easier way to do that than to have people come against each other based on their beliefs/religion? While we are busy defending our different "true" religion, Satan's running rampant and causing havoc and chaos in the world.

There is a saying by the late Wayne Dyer, "Change the way you look at things, and the things you look at change." For so long, we've looked at "religion" as a fight of whose religion is right and whose is wrong but at the end of the day, we are all on the same team when we look at the grand scheme of things. There is a fight between Yahuah and Satan; Satan wants to destroy us, while Yahuah is fighting to save us. Yahuah sent His Son, Yeshua, to die for our sins, regardless of what "religion" we practice. 1 John 3:8 tells us, *"The devil has been sinning since the beginning, so anyone who continues to sin belongs to the devil. Yeshua, Yahuah's Son came for this purpose: to destroy the devil's work"* (NCV). Matthew 20:28 also tells us, *"In the same way, the Son of Man did not come to be served. He came to serve others and to give his life as a ransom for many people"* (NCV).

Remember: Christianity is NOT a religion, it is a term used to refer to followers of Christ which means technically, Yeshua is not a Christian. He's Yeshua, Yahuah's Son and the *only* way to heaven because His death was the *only* way to defeat the devil. Yeshua did not come into the world to condemn the world, But to *SAVE* the world. Invite Him into your heart at this moment and you will be saved.

Chapter 12

Yeshua

*For Yahuah so loved the world, that he gave his only begotten
son, that whosoever believeth in him should not perish, but
have everlasting life ~ John 3:16 {KJV}*

❞ Long, after Noah died, not one of all the people that lived
on earth caught Yahuah's eyes till Abraham came along.
Abraham is the one that really impressed Yahuah and
Yahuah said, 'I'm going to do something really nice for him to
show him I appreciate the way he's living his life by upholding
my commands. I will make him the father of all nations.' So,
Yahuah made great promises to Abraham that he would bless
him financially and make his name great. Yahuah promised to

bless those who blessed Abraham and curse those who cursed him. Then He gave the greatest promise; that the entire world would be blessed because a Jewish Messiah would come through his seed who would deliver the world" (Taken from devotional email, Prime Time with Yahuah, "Yeshua: The Son of Abraham").

Most Christians think we have a monopoly on Yeshua, but if we want to get technical, Yeshua really "belongs" to the Jews, even if they don't want or acknowledge Him. Yeshua belongs to no one religion but to all humanity. When Adam and Eve opened the Pandora's Box of sin, they were not practicing Christianity, Islam, Judaism, or any other religion. They were just human beings who were friends of Yahuah; therefore, Yeshua came to close the box of sin for all people.

Matthew 9:36-38 tells us, *"But when he {Yeshua} saw the multitudes, he was moved with compassion on them, because they fainted, and were scattered abroad, as sheep having no shepherd. Then saith he unto his disciples, 'The harvest truly is plenteous, but the labourers are few; pray ye therefore Yahuah of the harvest, that he will send forth labourers into his harvest.'"* In other words, when Yeshua saw the crowds, He felt sorry for them because they were hurting and helpless, like sheep without shepherds. He told the disciples there were many people to "harvest" but only a few workers to help "harvest" them. Isn't what's going on in the world today reminiscent of what Yeshua saw back then? So many hurting people need Yeshua, but it's a shame that the "church" turns them away because they are sinners. Isn't the church supposed to bring sinners to Yeshua? Many churches have their own agendas and now preach messages of condemnation instead of inclusion. It is very possible to preach the word of Yahuah with love and not spew hate. If the sinners are not allowed to come to church, how can they change?

Yeshua' number one priority on earth was to make disciples of all the nations, as shown in Matthew 28:19, *"Go ye therefore, and teach all nations, baptizing them in the name of the Father, and of the Son, and of the Holy Ghost."* Let me emphasize that Scripture states to make disciples of ALL THE NATIONS and what do nations consists of? Blacks, atheists, whites, Jews, tall people, Muslims, Buddhists, short people, Sikhs, rich and poor people, sick and healthy people, gay people, adulterers, paedophiles, thieves, molesters, murderers, cheats, lesbians, transsexuals, mobsters, liars, homosexuals. I could go on but you get my point. Yeshua did not die for just the Christians; it was for all people, especially the sinners (1 John 2:1-2). The Bible even shows us that when Yeshua criticized people, His criticism was directed at the "religious" leaders because of their hypocrisy. We need to stop trying to put Yeshua into a "box of religion." Yeshua was a friend of sinners and people different from Him because that was His way of getting them to change their ways.

Do not let what the world has said about Yeshua (someone they know nothing about in my opinion) block your salvation because you've bought into the "Yeshua is from the Christianity religion." Yeshua is not from any religion, other than the religion of "visiting orphans and widows in their trouble and keeping himself unspotted from the world." Yeshua transcends religion, and He came for you, regardless of your nationality. He's most especially looking for the people playing on the dark side, the ones people have written off and given up on. You are the one He came for. Even if you are the devil or one of his minions, as long as you repent, accept and receive Him as your Saviour and open yourself to Him, He will answer your call and give you the Holy Spirit to guide you for the rest of your life on this earth (Acts 3:19). Invite Yeshua into your life today.

A PRAYER FOR REDEMPTION (from prayergear.com)
Yeshua, I hear You calling me. I feel You loving me. I know about Your ultimate sacrifice for me. I come to You just as I am and with all that I am. My sins violated the Father and I am so sorry. I repent of them and ask Your forgiveness. I love You because You are Love itself and You loved me first. I surrender my entire self and respond gratefully to Your invitation to live in You and have You live in me, now and forever. I pledge to You and announce to all that You are

My Saviour, Redeemer, Friend, Master and High Priest. Cover me with Your redemptive blood and fill me with Your Holy Spirit. Heal and transform me from being darkness to being light, the light of the world. I am willing to let Your Spirit take over every part of me and pray for Your grace to help me let go of self-indulgence, self-promotion, self-interest and rather make You the centre of my life and complete obedience to You, as Your servant, my passion. I know Your friends are to be my friends, and Your enemies are to be my own. Your ways will be mine. I know You will discipline me for my own spirit's sake. I accept all this while I embrace You and I'm nurtured by Your infinite love and mercy and sustained by my complete faith and trust in You, in the Father and the Holy Spirit. Come Yeshua; live in me as I live in You. I love You. I will follow You every day of my life, a life without end. Thank you for loving me into Your kingdom! Amen.

PS: Typically, when you accept Yeshua as your Saviour, you may not feel any different immediately but you will find out as time goes on, the things you used to do (sins), you no longer enjoy as it is no more your nature. Take for example an analogy given by Paul Washer. Imagine you were expecting someone and they showed up late, when you asked why they were late, they told you they had a flat tyre and as they were changing the tyre, the lug nut rolled into the street — they stepped in the street without looking and got hit by a logging truck weighing 30 tons, but there is no physical evidence to corroborate the story because they look the same. Will you believe them? Probably not, because you would expect them to at least look like they had an encounter with a 30-ton truck whether it's by looking dishevelled, having a few bruises or even a couple of broken bones. The same goes for when you have an encounter with Yahuah/Yeshua. Your life will change, you will not be the same person especially because the Holy Spirit now dwells within you and you now have the zeal for things of Yahuah. Ezekiel 36:27 tells us *"I will put my spirit within you, and cause you to walk in my statutes, and ye shall keep my judgments and do them."* There is no way you are "born again" and are not sensitive to the sin in your life. If you are not sensitive to sin to the point where you are making a conscious effort to stay away from it but in fact still enjoy sinning, you are kidding yourself, you are NOT born again.

Chapter 13

Sin

"...I want to do what is right, but I can't. I want to do what is good, but I don't. I don't want to do what is wrong, but I do it anyway" ~ Romans 7:18-19 (NLT)

Sin is an immoral act considered to be a transgression against Yahuah's Law. In today's society though, sin as we know it is being revamped into something people have a right to do; but in order to make law makers feel like they still have a bit of morals, they've made scapegoats of certain sins, such as drug dealing, abortion, homosexuality, murder, paedophilia, drunkenness, rape, and sometimes lying and theft. In the meantime, the world's fornicators, idolaters, cheaters, adulterers, sorcerers, the angry, the proud, the envious, the stingy, the greedy, and gluttons, etc. walk around freely to do whatever they want. What this has done to people in the free-to-roam category sin as I like to refer to them is, they believe they are better than the scapegoat sinners because their sin is not punishable by law. They fight to have the scapegoat sinners disciplined while they keep on sinning. How hypocritical! "The Bible teaches that homosexuality is a sin, but the Bible also teaches that pride is a sin, jealousy is a sin, and hate is a sin, evil thoughts are a sin. So I don't think that homosexuality and all these other scapegoat sins should be chosen as the overwhelming sin that we are doing today" (Billy Graham). By no means am I saying we shouldn't have laws. What I am saying is, if we are going to have laws on sins, we should have laws on all sins and not just some we feel should be punished. Sinning differently does not make us better than any other people who sin.

Why Does It Matter If We Sin?
Sin originated with the devil, which automatically makes it bad. The Bible tells us in John 8: 44, "*...He [the devil] was a murderer from the beginning. He has always hated the truth, because there is no truth in him. When he lies, it is consistent with his character; for he is a liar and the father of lies*" (NLT). We've found this to be true as well as found out over time (sometimes by personal experience) that sin brings about nothing but bad consequences and will eventually lead into the lake of fire and brimstone. You see, Yahuah would rather us not swim in a sea of pain, agony,

embarrassment, hurt, death, and all the negativity that comes with sin, so He sent His Son Yeshua to save us. It is now up to us to receive the gift of eternal life that He has for us. Unfortunately for us however, Yahuah is a gentleman and will not impose anything on us. We have to notify Him we are drowning, give Him permission to save us and then, He rescues us, dries us up, and clothe us with the linen of righteousness. He then makes sure we swim in the waters of love, peace, joy, longsuffering, gentleness, goodness, faith, meekness and temperance. The devil, on the other hand, is the opposite of Yahuah; he will impose on you and even force you to swim by coming to you as a friend. 2 Corinthians 11:14, 15 warn us, *"But I am not surprised! Even Satan disguises himself as an angel of light. So it is no wonder that his servants also disguise themselves as servants of righteousness. In the end they will get the punishment their wicked deeds deserve"* (NLT).

This hell thing is real and we have to protect ourselves from the devil and his antics. The devil knows his time as ruler on earth is coming to a wrap and he will soon be swimming in the lake of fire and brimstone, so he's working overtime to round up people to bring into the lake to suffer with him because he doesn't want to go down alone. He's sticking to his M.O and doing the same thing he did when he was banished from heaven—he took one-third of the angels with him. It really baffles me that most of us are ignorant of the devil and can't see his "hand" in everything. The devil has even been able to convince people that Yahuah is the "bad guy" because He wants to prevent people from doing bad things, if only we knew it was for our own good to follow Yahuah's command. Think about this, Yahuah didn't have to get involved after Adam and Eve got kicked out of the "Garden of Eden," He could have said, "You guys got yourselves into this mess, you figure it out." But He took it upon Himself to come up with ways, laws and principles that if followed would help us stay away from sins and produce good fruits in our lives. But what did we do instead? We resented Yahuah and instead of doing what's right, we jumped into the sea of sin, not understanding that our belief or lack of belief in Yahuah has no bearing on His existence.

Changes in the World's Viewpoints

One of the subtle yet effective things the devil — with the help of man — has been able to accomplish is changing people's viewpoints about sins and abominations. Our world has downplayed the consequences attached to these sins to make us comfortable, even though they are still very much sins and abominations to Yahuah.

• Contraceptives and masturbating are okay, but abortion isn't. Psalm 127:3 tells us, *"Lo, children are an heritage of the YAHUAH: and the fruit of the womb is his reward [sic]"* Every child is Yahuah's heritage, and every child belongs to Yahuah regardless of the circumstances surrounding the conception. Everyone screams pro-life, but what about the man or woman preventing a child from coming forth into the world by spilling his sperm outside of a woman and a woman on contraceptive?

Do you know this is the same as an abortion in Yahuah's eyes? It's not the killing of children alone that saddens Yahuah; it's also the prevention of His children from being conceived and coming into the world.

Genesis 38:6-10 tells the story of Onan, who married his dead brother's wife Tamar, to fulfil his duty to raise a child for his brother. Onan knew that the child would not be considered his, so every time he slept with Tamar, he spilled his semen on the ground to keep from providing a child for his brother. This incensed Yahuah for two reasons: 1) he refused to perform his duty of producing a child for his dead brother, a child who would have carried on his brother's name and 2) he prevented a child from coming into the world. So Yahuah killed him. We see people like the Duggars {19 Kids and Counting TV show} and scoff at them for having so many children, but in Yahuah's eyes, they've got it right (at least in that department). This is the reason you find several children born to parents when you go through the genealogy of different people in the Bible. Yahuah created sex for two reasons 1) to be enjoyed between a husband and wife 2) to procreate. Anything outside that is a misuse of sex. If you have sex and prevent any of Yahuah's children from coming into the world, you are as guilty as someone that's committed abortion. Crazy, huh? I know. I was like, *Are you kidding me?* When the Holy Spirit laid that one on my heart.

• Sodomy is one of the things that is an abomination to Yahuah because it's an unnatural use of the body (Leviticus 18:22 says *"Thou shalt not lie with mankind, as with womankind: it is abomination*). Any sexual act different from what Yahuah intended (sex between a man and woman) not only throws the body out of sync but it also throws things out of order in the world e.g. less number of men for women to marry and less number of children for Yahuah. It has and will always be man and woman in Yahuah's eyes yet people have failed to acknowledge this fact because they *feel* sodomy is a "loving" expression and they have a **right** to participate in it if they choose, which is true but I've learnt we should rarely rely on how we feel because it's been found out that most times what feels good to us is not always good for us no matter how much pleasure we derive from it.

• Fornication (whether straight or gay sex) is seen as harlotry and is an abomination in Yahuah's eyes. People have changed the viewpoint on this to liberating sex. At some point even in the carnal world, sex was only okay to engage in—at least openly—if you were in a relationship, but nowadays it's cool to give your body to whomever you see fit because most people are feeling liberated and believe they can do whatever they want with their body and to that I ask, liberated from what? 1 Corinthians 6:19-20 says, *"Don't you realise that your body is the temple of the Holy Spirit, who lives in you and was given to you by Yahuah? You do not belong to yourself, for Yahuah bought you with a high price. So you must honour Yahuah with your body"* (NLT). Instead, we delight in giving our bodies to different men and women and celebrate our whoredom. Oh, how Yahuah shakes His head at what this world has become. See, the people from past generations were sinners, but they still had limits. But we've evolved in our thinking and creativity and as these increased, our sins also increased. We've evolved and stepped into new territories of sin that were not around during our parents' and grandparents' days. Everything on Yahuah's lists of things that we are not supposed to do; we've done and continue to find ways to evolve in them. BUT, there is hope, and you know what that hope is? Your guilty conscience. Why is this good you ask? Because it means you can do better.

How to Know There's Still Hope

When you feel guilty about your sins, this means that there is a conflict between the body (flesh) and soul (spirit) i.e. the body wants to sin, but the spirit doesn't. This is usually when we should take a stand and not give in to the sin. However, most of us don't stop because we also enjoy the pleasure or perk the body (flesh) derives from the sin. The Bible tells us in Galatians 5:16-18, *"So I say, let the Holy Spirit guide your lives. Then you won't be doing what your sinful nature craves. The sinful nature wants to do evil, which is just the opposite of what the spirit wants. And the spirit gives us desires that are opposite of what the sinful nature desires. These two forces are constantly fighting each other, so you are not free to carry out your good intentions. But when you are directed by the Spirit, you are not under obligation to the Law of Moses"* {NLT}.

How to Deal with Sin

No matter what kinds of sin we are dealing with, we can conquer them with biblical solutions; we should begin to walk in the fear of Yahuah and the comfort and guidance of the Holy Spirit.

•   *Accept* that Yeshua already conquered sin which means you are no longer a slave to sin and if you do give in to temptation, *do not* let yourself get discouraged especially if you can't stop sinning immediately because when you do, you start to accept the sin as something that's part of you and make no effort to change. Instead begin to feel uncomfortable whenever you sin.

•   Change your habits: whatever sin you are involved in, stop putting yourself in the situation where you are likely to sin. If it means staying at home and directing your attention into something else, then do that. Pick up a hobby, do something different instead of giving in to that sin. You may fall but once you start resisting, it will let up. You see, sin is a bully and once you stand up to a bully, it doesn't like you anymore, you've become too much work and sin does not like to work for its people. Sin looks for people that WANT to sin and once you start resisting, it's out. What better way to stay away from that sin but by doing something you enjoy and is fun. Sounds silly I know but pick something you've always wanted to do and make it a goal to do that thing at an expert level after a certain amount of time (I would suggest a year, six months if you're being ambitious). Try out in a singing, dancing, or acting competition; learn to fly a plane, learn to cook and/or bake (both male and female can do this); engage in carpentry or masonry; learn to do hair, sew, knit; there are so many things you can engage in but most importantly, let the Holy Spirit guide you.

***

Judgment

Depending on whom you speak with, some people tell you we are not to judge, while some people say it's our right to judge. I believe one of the reasons people, especially believers, are adamant on not judging is because we are comfortable in our sins and want to continue sinning. If we know a believer who openly sins, it helps our case and we use it to justify our own sins. But I've started to see things differently and I pray other followers of Christ would start to see things this way, too. When this world passes away, I want to spend eternity, not in the lake of fire and brimstone but in the New Jerusalem. Revelation 21:27 tells us, *"Nothing evil will be allowed to enter, nor anyone who practices shameful idolatry and dishonesty but only those whose names are written in the Lamb's Book of Life"* (NLT). While dying to sin every day is no easy task, we know Yeshua died for our sins and for that reason, we as followers of Christ have no obligation to do what our sinful nature urges us to do. 2 Corinthians 5:17 tells us *"Therefore if any man be in Christ, he is a new creature: old things are passed away; behold all things are become new."* That means all the sins, pain, debt, character flaws, sickness and diseases, generational curses, worry, doubt, anxiety, lack etc. are all in the past. They died with Yeshua. If we truly believe Yeshua died for our sins, then we should believe our past is just that—our past, nothing more—which means we are no more sinners. Yes we may still fall and sin but we should not identify as sinners. Every time we call ourselves sinners, we nail Yeshua back to that cross. We should believe we are now new creatures with the goal of walking in the Spirit and shunning sin. In other words, we are controlled by our spirit and not our flesh, so if and when we sin, we should want to be held accountable and judged, i.e. the error of our ways called out in love by other believers. That way, we can confess our sins to Yahuah and not continue sinning.

***

What I've found out from reading the Bible is that, a word has more than one meaning and the Bible should NEVER be read without a concordance e.g. Strong's. The reason is so you're sure you have the right meaning and interpretation and not the most common meaning and wrong interpretations out there. Most times, we use the most *common* interpretation for a word which in turn presents the *wrong* meaning. The word judgement is one of those words. Judge in the concordance means: to *distinguish i.e. to decide (mentally or judicially; by implication, to try, condemn, punish: avenge, conclude, condemn, damn, decree, determine, esteem, judge (sue at the) law, ordain, call in question, sentence, to think).* We see here there are different meanings to this word. The problem nowadays is most people do not understand there are several meanings and mainly use just the common meaning, *condemnation.*

Let's see what Yeshua had to say about judgment in Matthew 7:1-5, *"Judge not, that ye be not judged. For with that judgment ye judge, ye shall be judged: and with what measure ye mete, it shall be measured to you again. And why beholdest thou the mote that is in thy brother's eye, but considerest not the beam that is in thine own eye? Or how wilt thou say to thy brother, let me pull out the mote out of thine eye; and behold, a beam is in thine own eye? Thou hypocrite, first cast out the beam out of thine own eye; and then shalt thou see clearly to cast out the mote out of thy brother's eye."* We see in verses 1-4, Yeshua is talking about people who judge (condemn). He warns them against being hypocrites, especially when they also sin. Yeshua reminds them they will also go through "trial" on Judgment Day and the same intensity and reasoning application they invested when condemning other people will be the same intensity used on them during their "trial." Verse 5, however, says, *"Then you will see clearly to remove the speck from your brother's eyes."* This shows us we can judge i.e. call out the error of their ways—as long as we do this in love and are not being hypocritical. Galatians 6:1 further explains, *"Brothers, if anyone is caught in any sin, you who are spiritual [that is, you who are responsive to the guidance of the Spirit] are to restore such a person in a spirit of gentleness [not with a sense of superiority or self-righteousness], keeping a watchful eye on yourself, so that you are not tempted as well"*[AMP]. In other words, our job as followers of Christ is to let the person know gently and with love that whatever they might be doing is classed as sin. We share Yahuah's Word with them and let the Holy Spirit do its job of convicting that person. We don't need to condemn and berate.

Another thing we have to pay close attention to when we are in judging mode (whether condemnation or calling out in love) is our motives and intentions. Are we calling into question someone's sins because we want the best for them and we don't want this sin to stop them from going through the pearly gates? Or are we doing it because we're feeling "holier than thou" and want to show how immoral the other person is? If it's the first reason, we will always approach them with compassion and if they still don't get it, all you can do is pray for them and move on. If it's the latter, however, we get all worked up because we want to prove a point and show how much of a sinner they are.

Can We Judge Everyone?

Most of us believers are quick to spot sinners and want to condemn them because we feel they are immoral and we are the epitome of morality. However, read what Brother Paul (as I like to refer to him) had to say in 1 Corinthians 5:9-13, *"When I wrote to you before, I told you not to associate with people who indulge in sexual sin. But I wasn't talking about unbelievers who indulge in sexual sin, or are greedy, or cheat people, or worship idols. You would have to leave this world to avoid people like that. I meant that you are not to associate with anyone who claims to be a believer yet indulges in sexual sin, or is greedy, or worship idols, or is abusive, or is a* drunkard, or cheats people. Don't even eat with such people. It isn't my responsibility to judge (call in to question) outsiders, but it is certainly is your responsibility to judge (call in to question) those inside the church who are sinning" (NLT). I totally agree with his view and I believe the right way to restore a sinner is gently. In I.H. Plemmons' poem *Judge Gently*, he writes, "Don't be too harsh with the man that sins or pelt him with words or stone unless you are sure—yea, doubly sure that you have no sins of your own for you know if the tempter's voice should whisper as soft to you as it did to him when he went astray, it might cause you to falter too."

I believe the biggest takeaway about judgment is, whether you believe you should judge (call into question/condemn) or not, remember this: should you choose to judge (condemn), remember what Yeshua says in Matthew 7: 2: "*You will be judged in the same way that you judge others, and the amount you give to others will be given to you*" (NCV).

***

False Prophets (By Their Fruits, You Shall Know Them)

Yeshua warns in Matthew 7:15-19, "*Beware of false prophets, who come to you in sheep's clothing, but inwardly they are ravenous wolves. You will know them by their fruits. Do men gather grapes from thorn bushes or figs from thistles? Even so, every good tree bears good fruit, but a bad tree bears bad fruit. A good tree cannot bear bad fruit, nor can a bad tree bear good fruit. Every tree that does not bear good fruit is cut down and thrown into the fire. Therefore by their fruits you will know them"* (NKJV).

In some situations, it seems being a pastor, preacher, etc. has become a get-rich-quick hustle — there are churches on every corner you turn. The church industry (if there's anything like that) is so saturated that you can't tell the real from the fake. What I've observed, however, is we usually toss people into the fake category based on their level of wealth. I even read where someone said a dead giveaway of knowing a "fake" pastor is if the pastor owns a private jet. Really? How absurd! Some people justify this line of thinking by saying Yeshua was a simple guy without any material wealth, so any wealthy Christian automatically equates to fake. The truth of the matter is all these religious heads are humans just like you and me, just because they've been called to serve Yahuah does not mean they will automatically stop liking nice things. In fact, I think it's quite the opposite. If they liked nice things before they began preaching, they might like them even more, especially if Yahuah has blessed them with the opportunities to become wealthy.

It's unfair to categorize someone based on their earthly possessions, especially since we don't know how they are helping to advance Yahuah's Kingdom financially. Because they don't scream it in church every Sunday does not mean they don't help people out and even if they don't, they will have to give account on Judgment Day since one of the conditions of Yahuah blessing people financially is so they can be a blessing to other people. We can't judge people for what they have and how we believe they should use it, especially if given the opportunities ourselves, we might do even worse. I say all this to stress the fact that if a pastor can afford to purchase a plane, who are we to decide what he uses his money for? Yes, Yeshua lived a simple life because that's what He chose and wanted to do. It's amazing how we pick and choose when to use Yeshua as a measuring stick. When we're talking about ourselves, we say such things as, "I can't be like Yeshua because He is Yahuah's Son and the only perfect being that ever lived. I can't come close." Yet when it's time to criticize someone for his or her wealth, we use Yeshua. Hypocrite much?!

Anyone who knows Yahuah and how He works knows He wants us to live life abundantly in every area of our lives. Yes, even in the area of finances, which is why He blessed the likes of Abraham, Isaac, Jacob, Joseph, King David, King Solomon, Job, etc. with great wealth. With that said, I DO NOT AGREE with the focus on material wealth that has taken hold of the Church. We have lost our focus on what our assignment as followers of Christ is and are consumed with money, wealth, and material things. Matthew 6:24 says, *"No man can serve two masters: for either he will hate the one, and love the other; or else he will hold to the one, and despise the other. Ye cannot serve Yahuah and Mammon."* This focus on mammon, material wealth, is not what Yeshua commanded us to do. The focus of the Body of Christ should be advancing the Kingdom of Yahuah and nothing else (see Matthew 28:19-20).

Unfortunately, we live in times just like Brother Paul wrote about in Romans 16:17,18, *"Now I beseech you, brethren, mark them which cause divisions and offences contrary to the doctrine which ye have learned; and avoid them. For they that are such serve not Yeshua, but their own belly; and by good words and fair speeches deceive the hearts of the simple."* Some preachers today are being politically correct, deviating from the Bible, adding to the Bible, and/or twisting the Bible to make their messages fit into what the "world" wants to hear. Like Paul Washer says "One of the greatest distinguishing marks of a false prophet is that he will always tell you what you want to hear, he will never rain on your parade; he will get you clapping, he will get you jumping, he will keep you entertained, and he will present a Christianity to you that will make your church look like a six flags over Yeshua." This is how some of them have been able to misrepresent an important biblical concept of Yahuah's *grace.*

***

Grace

Many preachers have distorted the true message of grace, and they do that by quoting Romans 5:19 -21, *"One man [Adam] disobeyed Yahuah, and many become sinners. In the same way, one man [Yeshua] obeyed Yahuah, and many will be made right. The law came to make sin worse, but when sin grew worse, Yahuah's grace increased. Sin once used death to rule us, but Yahuah gave people more of his grace so that grace could rule by making people right with him. And this brings life forever through Yeshua"* (NCV). And they stop reading Scripture there without going on to the next verse, so people use this as a license to go on sinning. But what does the Bible say when you flip to the next chapter and read Romans 6:1-7, *"What shall we say then? Shall we continue in sin that grace may abound? Certainly not! How shall we who died to sin live any longer in it? Or do you not know that as many of us as were baptized into Christ Yeshua were baptized into His death? Therefore we were buried with Him through baptism into death, that just as Christ was raised from the dead by the glory of the Father, even so we also should walk in newness of life. For if we have been united together in the likeness of His death, certainly we also shall be in the likeness of His resurrection, knowing this, that our old man was crucified with Him, that the body of sin might be done away with, that we should no longer be slaves of sin. For he who has died has been freed from sin"* (NKJV). This tells us grace as Yahuah intended it was not given to us as a license to sin or continue to sin. Grace was given to set us free from sin.

Identifying False Prophets

Yahuah knew we would eventually get to end times with false prophets running rampant, so He laid out instructions in His Word on how we can weed them out. First, read His Word. If you don't know what He says, you won't be able to discern whether what you are being told is biblical or something the pastor has embraced as Yahuah's words because it helps his/her agenda. For example, some pastors use these lines: "Let the weak say I am strong and let the poor say I am rich because of what the Lord has done." Pastors use these words as if they're in Scripture, but they're not. They come from a great song but not from the Bible. A lot of pastors take that line and run with it because it helps their cause of receiving money.

The second way to detect false prophets is to test the spirit. This is probably the best advice Yahuah gave us when it comes to discerning whether He's asking us to do something. Yahuah's Word NEVER changes. He won't tell us not to have premarital sex, and then say it's okay to use a condom when doing it. No! Many times the reason we can't test the spirit is that we don't know what He said in His Word. Consequently, we accept anything we hear as Yahuah's Word when really it's a seducing spirit from the enemy, and we fall hook line and sinker. Please, do yourself a favour, *READ THE WORD* for yourself and *test all spirits*.

The third way to test for false prophets is the fruit. By their FRUITS you shall know them, as Yeshua said in Matthew 7:16. About pastors and other Christian leaders, we must ask ourselves, do they believe that Yeshua is the only way to get through to the Father and are they obedient to Yeshua and teaching what He commanded? Are they concerned about your soul (teaching about salvation) or more concerned about how you will be financially prosperous? Are they sharing the message of love and inclusion or hate and division? No matter how great the sin, Yeshua never excluded anyone from forgiveness and love. He tells us in Mark 2:17, "...*They that are whole have no need of the physician, but they that are sick: I came not to call the righteous but sinners to repentance."* Preachers should welcome sinners, especially the ones in the scapegoat category and teach them how to come out of their sin instead of berating and condemning them in every Bible sermon. Yeshua says in John 13: 34-35, *"A new commandment I give unto you, that ye love one another; as I have loved you, that ye also love one another. By this shall all men know that ye are my disciples, if ye have love one to another."* Only by loving one another will we evidently be Yeshua's followers.

Pastors, preachers, priests and other church leaders are all like "trees" of their religious sects. So one of the questions you have to ask about your pastor is what type of tree is he or she? Are they producing the right elements for the branches to also bear fruit i.e. spiritual fruit, divine health and healing, financial blessing etc.? Is the congregation also abundantly blessed in every area the pastor is blessed in? If it's just the pastor that is blessed, it's a **BIG RED FLAG**. If Yahuah is blessing the pastor especially financially (who by the way is supposed to be the root of the tree and as the root is the provider of water and other inorganic nutrients to the branches), the pastor's blessings should in turn apply to his congregation. The only reason this would not be happening is if there's really no anointing on this pastor's life and the financial abundance he/she is enjoying is not from Yahuah but from his/her unsuspecting congregation. If this is the situation at your place of worship, I recommend you break your branch and attach yourself to another flourishing tree i.e. another church.

Chapter 14

Tithe and Offering

*"Give freely and become more wealthy; be stingy and lose
everything" ~ Proverbs 11:24*

Tithing *was* a compulsory offering that required the
Israelites to give ten percent of their firstfruits because
Yahuah provided the harvest. This first part was
returned to Him to show appreciation for Him blessing them
and not paying tithe back then was considered robbing Yahuah
as told in Malachi 3:8-9, *"Should people cheat Yahuah? Yet you have
cheated me! But you ask, 'What do you mean? When did we ever cheat
you?' You have cheated me of the tithes and offerings due to me. You*

are under a curse, for your whole nation has been cheating me" (NLT).

We see several people in the Bible tithe and give offerings out of the abundance Yahuah provided for them. For example, Jacob promised to give tithes to Yahuah. Genesis 28:20-22 says, *"Then Jacob made this vow: 'If Yahuah will indeed be with me and protect me on this journey, and if he will provide me with food and clothing, and if I return safely to my father's home, then Yahuah will certainly be my God. And this memorial pillar I have set up will become a place for worshipping Yahuah, and I will present to Him a tenth of everything He gives me.'"* Mark 12:41-44 tells of the story of the "Widow's Mite." *"Yeshua sat down near the collection box in the Temple and watched as the crowds dropped in their money. Many rich people put in large amounts. Then a poor widow came and dropped in two small coins. Yeshua called his disciples to him and said, 'I tell you the truth, this poor widow has given more than all the others who are making contributions. For they gave a tiny part of their surplus, but she, poor as she is, has given everything she had to live on.'"* We also see the story of the Pharisee and Tax Collector in Luke 18:9-14. The Pharisee said as he prayed, *"...I fast twice a week, and I give a tenth of my income."*

My belief is, before Yeshua hung for our sins, we were **required** to tithe but after His resurrection, **we are no longer required to**. 2 Corinthians 9:7 says, *"Every man according as he purposeth in his heart, so let him give; not grudgingly, or of necessity: for Yahuah loveth a cheerful giver."* In order words, *"You must each decide in your heart how much to give. And don't give reluctantly or* in response to pressure. For Yahuah loves a person who gives cheerfully" (NLT). BUT I STILL TITHE. Tithing, to me, is one of the best laws Yahuah put forth. It is also one if not the one time He asked that we test Him. Malachi 3:10-12 states, "'*Bring all the tithes into the storehouse so there will be enough food in my Temple. If you do,' says Yahuah, 'I will open the windows of heaven for you. I will pour out a blessing so great that you won't have enough room to take it in! Try it! Put me to the test! Your crops will be abundant, for I will guard them from insects and disease. Your grapes will not fall from the vine before they are ripe,' says Yahuah. 'Then all nations will call you blessed, for your land will be such a delight,' says Yahuah.*" I tithe because there are blessings attached to tithing and who wouldn't want such blessings? If you have been tithing yet, you are not experiencing what Yahuah promised in regards to tithing, you may be tithing the wrong way.

The Order in which You Tithe Matters

Proverbs 3:9-10 says, "*Honour Yahuah with thy substance, and with the firstfruits of all thine increase: so shall thy barns be filled with plenty, and thy presses shall burst out with new wine*" or as translated in the NLT, "*Honour Yahuah with your wealth and with the best part of everything you produce. Then he will fill your barns with grain, and your vats will overflow with good wine.*" Most people set their tithe aside (so they don't spend it) till the next time they are in church, then they pay it but in the meantime, they've already spent the increase they are tithing on. The tithe is the *firstfruit* i.e. the first portion so Yahuah should get his portion first—that way, He can bless the remainder of the increase but most people pay their 'tithe' after the increase is well spent which defeats the purpose of tithing. We have to make sure our tithe is received by Yahuah before we start to spend any of the increase, so pay it online or set direct deposit; whichever way works for you, just make sure Yahuah gets His portion first so he can bless the remainder. The order in which we pay our tithe matters.

Who You Tithe and Give Offerings through Matter
Your *covering* matters, that is, the person you choose to lead you matters. The church you pay your tithe to matters. Are you being properly discipled? Is your Pastor, Preacher, Apostle, Reverend, etc. following Yahuah's commands? Are they using the money for good? Are they taking care of the orphans and widows as Yahuah instructed? Are they taking care of the poor? Are they accountable for their actions when they fall? Maybe you have one of those pastors that think they are untouchable because they know most of their congregants 'worship' them and no matter what happens, you follow them blindly and have their backs even when the truth is screaming in your face. You should know that, if your "covering" is cursed, so are you. Malachi 3:9 says, *"You are under a curse, for your whole nation has been cheating me."* If your covering is not following Yahuah's commands, He might have cursed them and you could be putting yourself under a curse, too.

Again, tithing is no longer required of the followers of Christ but *"Remember this – a farmer who plants only a few seeds*

Bolanle Pacheco

will get a small crop. But the one who plants generously will get a generous crop" 2 Corinthians 9:6 (NLT).

Chapter 15

Money

But they that will be rich fall into temptation and a snare, and into many foolish and hurtful lusts which drown men in destruction and perdition. For the LOVE OF MONEY is the root of all evil: which some coveted after, they have erred from the faith, and pierced themselves through with many sorrows ~ 1 Timothy 6:9-10

Many of us have heard the above verse used many times but mostly in the wrong way. People typically say, "Money is the root of all evil," but this is not biblically true. Money is NOT the root of all evil; Scripture tells us the "LOVE OF MONEY" is the culprit here.

If you love money to the point that it is all you breathe, work, think and do anything for, that's when it becomes a problem. There are plenty of people who don't "chase" money but still earn lots of it (typically, how it operates in Yahuah's Kingdom) i.e. the people who aren't focused on money are the ones who end up making lots of it. Money mostly eludes those who want it above all else and they end up chasing it all their lives. In the case of the people who do catch up with it, they can't enjoy it because they are so consumed by not losing their earnings, so they work harder to get more of it. These people, however, are never satisfied.

The Scriptures tell us that focusing on money can become a real problem. 1 Timothy 6:10 says, "*...Which while some have coveted after, they have erred from the faith and pierced themselves through with many sorrows.*" We live in a world where we are all in love with money and are hungry for material things. We think of the cars, houses, designer clothes, shoes, bags, and all the extracurricular activities we can partake in with money, to the extent we don't even know when we start to lower our morals and integrity. We've become so money hungry that even when we know we are dipping our toes in questionable waters, we justify our actions to ourselves and others because we can't bear to let the money go and before we know it, we are swimming with sharks. We end up suffering negative consequences we could have avoided if we hadn't compromised our morals and integrity. In essence, *we* pierced ourselves through sorrow, no one else did that. We did that; all for the love of money.

Money Lovers

The devil will use money as a trap to catch Yahuah's people but in most cases, he doesn't even have to lift a finger to tempt us; our own love of money fuels the desire so all the devil has to do is give us an illusion of money such as the next big deal, to keep us going but it never comes into fruition. There are times the devil will even have us come into money e.g. lottery winnings, new higher paying jobs, new business deal, etc. because he knows it will shift our focus from the things of Yahuah.

I loved money so much it was all I lived for, but I always seemed to fall short of earning the amount of money I wanted and it wasn't for lack of effort because I worked my butt off in the real estate market for eight years. While I was very comfortable, I could never reach the kind of success I saw other top real estate agents achieve. It seemed I was always one deal short, or I'd lose one deal here, another there. It was frustrating to say the least. Business really fell off for me after I got pregnant and had Evan. Mentally, I had gotten to a desperate state financially and I was starting to unravel. I had been praying to Yahuah to show me a way to make money — ironic, right? Anyway I had been sitting outside in the backyard when the story of the disciples fishing came to mind. This story can be found in John 21:3-6 & Luke 5:4-8. The disciples had been fishing a long while and had caught nothing; Yeshua came by and asked them to cast their nets again at the same spot. They didn't want to, but eventually gave in. They cast their net and this time around, they caught so many fish their nets were bursting. Then the story of finding a coin in a fish came to me from Matthew 17:24-27. Taxes were due; Yeshua asked peter to go fish and inside that fish would be a coin that would pay taxes for not just Peter but also Yeshua's. I received these Scriptures in my spirit. Then I got up to go inside.

I had barely gotten up, when a call about how to make a bulk load of money came through on my cell phone and I just knew it was Yahuah who sent it to me. How could it not be?! I had just thought of the stories in the Bible that pointed to that. I listened to the pitch, and I was excited but there was something missing. In the stories I had just remembered, Yeshua showed where and how. If this was what Yahuah was asking me to do, why hadn't He provided the "how" like He had provided for Peter? I didn't have the capital to start this business.

I went to my room to pray and thanked Yahuah for answering my prayers. I woke up the next morning eager about this business and prayed again but nothing; as Yahuah was silent. In my impatience, I decided to "help" Yahuah since I saw the potential of how much money I could make. I resorted to borrowing money from my sister Dotun by lying to her about our finances (I exaggerated our financial situation and told her it was dire) and she gave me the money a couple of days later. I invested the money in the business, and dove right in. I worked nine to ten hours a day; working so hard the "owner" hired me to make his own calls. He gave me a great deal and I took it.

From each sale he made, he agreed he would pay me $500. I kept making calls and the more people I talked to, the more I started to get an inclination this was sort of a "legal" scam. People kept on saying the services didn't work the way it had been advertised, then it occurred to me *it's the same thing for me.* I was sold something and it's not working the way it was advertised. I hit the sad realisation: I had sunk my investment. I was devastated that I had fallen for a scam all in the name of making some quick money. But I saw the silver lining; the owner said he would pay me $500 for all the phone calls I had been making. While it was nothing compared to what I invested, it was better than nothing. I woke up about three days later and saw he had deposited the money in my account. I went to the bank, took the money out and closed that account. I cancelled my membership with the company and vowed never to chase money again.

I didn't know what to do with myself, if I didn't have to chase money. I kept praying to Yahuah, asking Him what He wanted me to do. When the Holy Spirit finally spoke to me, this is how the conversation went.

Holy Spirit: You are to become a homemaker aka Stayhomepreneur.

Me: A what?

Holy Spirit: A housewife, homemaker, stay-at-home mom, business owner like the Proverbs 31 woman.

Me: Heck, No! (I burst out, before I realised I blurted that out.) I'm sorry, I didn't go to school and work this hard in my career

to become a housewife. For Christ's sake, I was the epitome of
Ms. Independent (When Neyo's song Ms. Independent was in
circulation, a lot of people told me they always thought of me
whenever that song came on). How do I go from Ms.
Independent to a housewife?! I think not. Why would I want to
do that?

Holy Spirit: So you can focus on your family and the
assignment Yahuah has for you.

Me: Okaaaay, and what assignment is that?

Holy Spirit: Write the book Yahuah has been putting on your
heart. You have the time now, you're already home with Evan.
Quit real estate and focus on being the woman Yahuah has
ordained you to be; you will live a happier life, and it will help
you to be a more understanding wife, mother, daughter, friend,
etc. Most importantly, you will be advancing Yahuah's
Kingdom.

Me: (in an almost crying voice) But I don't want to be a
housewife. I won't have any money and will be forced to
depend on Abayomi (before I could finish, I heard the Holy
Spirit say...)

Holy Spirit: No, you will have to depend on Yahuah for
EVERYTHING. Yahuah will provide for Abayomi and give him
the reward due to him as promised in Proverbs 18:22, *"Whoso
findeth a wife, findeth a good thing, and obtaineth Yahuah's favour."*
Do you think he has received that blessing?

Me: I don't believe so.

Holy Spirit: Haven't you wondered why he hasn't?

Me: I'm guessing you're about to tell me.

Holy Spirit: In order for a husband to obtain the Proverbs 18: 22 blessing, he has to have a wife who lives by heavenly standards, one who is practicing the biblical principles of marriage. This is not a reward the husband only benefits from; Yahuah will also reward you for your obedience. Being a housewife does not mean you will be idle; in fact quite the opposite (Read Proverbs 31:10 -31). Yahuah will raise you up with your own "business" as He's blessed EVERY woman with an entrepreneurial spirit; Yahuah will send you on "missions" to harvest souls for the Kingdom. Your mind cannot fathom what He is going to do. You will be "working," but your family will be your number one priority because ultimately this is Yahuah's purpose for you as a wife. He made men to protect, provide and lead the family so that you (woman) can be soft and vulnerable because you are the nurturer, the glue that holds the family together. When you are absent and away at work, don't kid yourself, your family is "suffering" — you don't get to spend quality time with them and you're not there to be your husband's solace (what Yahuah made you for) especially when he comes back from a hard day's work because you're wound tight, too as you've also had a hard day at work and you're hardly there to raise your kids (purpose of being a mother). It will not be an easy path to go down — you will have to rely heavily on Yahuah for everything, especially your finances. It will be challenging and foreign to you in the beginning, but know that I WILL ALWAYS BE THERE to guide you. Yahuah has put things money cannot quantify in women especially in her *HANDS* and when she uses her hands to create, beautiful things happen. When a woman becomes a wife and lives according to Yahuah's commands, two things happen: 1} the husband gets his reward 2} Yahuah's SPECIAL assignment for you as a wife is revealed.

I wasn't really convinced, or should I say, I wasn't ready to give up my career and be a stay-at-home mom. So I figured I could pull a fast one by continuing to dabble in real estate as well as being a stay-at-home mom and not heed what the Holy Spirit told me. But nothing went right after that. All the deals I had under contract and was relying on to carry me through the transition period somehow fell through. I started tapping into my savings till I was tapped out with no money coming in. Aaarrrrggghhhhh!!!

***

One day I went to Costco to get some tilapia and seaweed salad and it came to about $23, I handed the cashier my Visa credit card but unbeknownst to me, they only accepted debit cards and AMEX. What? No credit cards? I didn't have $23 in my bank account, so I couldn't use my debit card. I was upset I had driven all the way and couldn't even get what I needed. I didn't even know when the tears started flowing; I was at my wits end. How could I not have $23 in my account? How did I go from being financially comfortable to not having any money in my account? I cried all the way home. Then I started to put things in perspective. While I personally might have been broke, Abayomi wasn't broke. I was so independent minded that I had forgotten I had a partner who Yahuah was providing for so he could in turn provide for me when I couldn't. I realised I had come to a point in my marriage where I had to let my husband provide and take care of me and also trust that he wouldn't mistreat me because he is providing for me like we are told men do when they are the providers. All the worry and anxiety I was feeling were all a figment of my imagination. I had jumped on the bandwagon of worry and rode that train all around, letting my negative perspective get me to the point of desperation, a place that was not our reality.

I made a decision I was really done chasing money this time around, and I meant it. I was going to focus on writing "the book" and let Yahuah take it from there. Yahuah looks at your heart and knows when you're sincere but I believe the enemy does too. The enemy knows when he's about to lose someone he's had in his grips for a long time and he will not back down without a fight. This is why he tried to attack my mind the very first time I made a decision to walk in my purpose. Like I said earlier, the devil will not bother you when you are not following Yahuah's ways, but start doing Yahuah's will and the attacks will start. Satan is very territorial and wants to rule over our lives by something he knows we need—we all need money and anyone who says we don't is someone with a lot of it. Most of us make the mistake of chasing it by doing something that's all about how much we can make, instead of what we love to do (our passion) that will in turn bring us money. This is the reason why no matter how much money you have, you will never be happy unless you're doing something you love. Money is energy, and as long as you are working on your assignment from Yahuah, i.e. your purpose, money will come to you. Proverbs 10:22 says *"The blessing of Yahuah, it maketh rich and he addeth no sorrow with it."*

Debt

I can't close this chapter without speaking about debt. Debt as we all know brings nothing more than negative consequences. Think about it; do you know anyone who has had a positive debt experience? Most of us, especially if we live in the western world, have credit cards, mortgages, car notes, etc. We've been programmed to think without "credit," we are at a disadvantage because you can only buy things when you have the cash. I'm not going to deny that credit makes things seem easier upfront but in the long run, it's nothing but a hassle. Being able to buy things on credit has done nothing more than give people the wrong indication of their financial status. By getting into debt so many people have willingly joined the "new form of slavery."

The Bible says in Romans 13:8 *"Owe no man anything but to love one another..."* and in Proverbs 22:7, *"The rich ruleth over the poor, and the borrower is servant to the lender."* When you put yourself in debt, you've put yourself under Satan's rule and you have to be prepared for when it's time to pay up for those things you enjoyed on credit (Trust me; I know it all too well, as I've been there). Debt pulls us away from Yahuah's Kingdom because we're too busy worrying about money and how to get more of it, leaving us without time to focus on Yahuah. We need to get rid of debt by making sure we save and only buy things when we can afford to pay cash for it, which means we have to change our lifestyles by not keeping up with the Joneses' and cutting our coats according to the amount of fabric we have — that is, based on what we can afford and not what we want.

Chapter 16

Marriage Principles

For this cause shall a man leave father and mother, and shall cleave to his wife: and they twain shall be one flesh? Wherefore they are no more twain, but one flesh. What therefore Yahuah hath joined together, let not man put asunder ~ Matthew 19:5-6

DISCLAIMER! I must preface this chapter by saying most people will disagree with things I say in this chapter, especially feminists, but keep in mind, I did not write/inspire the Bible, Yahuah did. I'm regurgitating biblical principles.

Marriage according to Yahuah is the cleaving and uniting of a male and a female who make a covenant (agreement which cannot be broken) to commit their lives to remain together until death. These principles are found in (Matthew 19.1-12), Mark 10:6-9, *"But from the beginning of the creation Yahuah made them male and female. For this cause shall a man leave his father and mother, and cleave to his wife; and they twain shall be one flesh: so then they are no more twain, but one flesh. What therefore Yahuah hath joined together, let not man put asunder."* The Bible further tells us in Romans 7:2, *"...When a woman marries, the law binds her to her husband as long as he is alive. But if he dies, the laws of marriage no longer apply to her"* (NLT) and vice versa. This tells us that marriage as Yahuah intended is supposed to last forever and the only situation that can separate the covenant of marriage is death.

What Are Yahuah's Intended Purposes for Marriage?

The marriage relationship was the first human institution established by Yahuah. In Genesis 2:18, we find the account of the creation of Adam and Eve, ***"And Yahuah said, 'It is not good that the man should be alone; I will make him an help meet for him'"*** [Sic]. We see that Yahuah made woman to meet Adam's needs for companionship, as well as an aide. He then made Adam and Eve become "one flesh" in order to serve and exalt Him as told in Malachi 2:15, *"Didn't YAHUAH make you one with your wife? In body and spirit you are his. And what does he want? Godly children from your union so guard your heart; remain loyal to the wife of your youth"* (NLT). This relationship was designed like the relationship Yahuah has with mankind—He is our king and we are His subjects. Likewise, in marriage, the husband is the head of the wife (Ephesians 5:23) and the woman is the helpmeet (suitable aide). Marriage is *not* a partnership, as it's so often expressed and practiced in the"world". The only aspect of marriage that makes it a partnership is the number of people in it. (Wives, this does not suggest that Yahuah sees us as less than the man; not at all). Our spirit is equal to that of a man's in the heavenly realm, but the role we play in the physical world is what makes us different. Let's look at those differences in roles.

Biblical Roles of Husband

Yahuah's main roles for the husband are for him to be a leader, provider, and protector.

Leader — In 1 Corinthians 11:3 (NASB), Yahuah lays out a chain of command, *"But I want you to understand that Christ is the head of every man, and the man is the head of a woman, and Yahuah is the head of Christ"* (NASB; see also Ephesians 5:23 and Matthew 19: 5-6). In Mark 10:7, Yeshua says, *"For this cause shall a man leave his father and mother and cleave to his wife."* This means the man is now the head of his household and attached to his wife. No one except Yahuah has the authority over his home, so whatever the husband says is final, not what his mother or any other family member says. FYI — even though Yahuah gave the husband the position of leadership in the marriage, he did not give him the authority to oppress his wife (as we sometimes see husbands do) but instead to love and lead like Yeshua. Ephesians 5:25-26 says, *"Husbands, love your wives, even as Christ also loved the church and gave himself for it; that he might sanctify and cleanse it with the washing of water by the word."*

Yahuah wants a husband to have the ultimate kind of love for his wife. Ephesians 5:28, 29 reads, *"So ought men to love their wives as their own bodies. He that loveth his wife loveth himself. For no man ever yet hated his own flesh; but nourisheth and cherisheth it, even as unto Yahuah."* A man should stand up for his wife (unless of course she's wrong; you don't want to co-sign wrong behaviour) but even at that, he should not allow anyone **especially his mother**, to bully his wife. A wife is part of the husband and should be treated as such. You should treat your wife the way you treat yourself. What you won't do to yourself, you shouldn't do to your wife.

Breadwinner and Provider — Two Scriptures point us to the provider role of a husband.

Genesis 3: 17-19, *"And unto Adam he said, 'Because thou hast hearkened unto the voice of thy wife, and hast eaten of the tree, of which I commanded thee, saying, 'Thou shalt not eat of it: cursed is the ground for thy sake; in sorrow shalt thou eat of it all the days of thy life; thorns also and thistles shall it bring forth to thee; and thou shalt eat the herb of the field; in the sweat of thy face shalt thou eat bread, till thou return unto the ground; for out of it wast thou taken: for dust thou art, and unto dust shalt thou return.'"*

1 Timothy 5:8, "*But if any provide not for his own, and specially for those of his house, he hath denied the faith, and is worse than an infidel [sic].*"

Protector — one of the main roles of husbands is that of protectors. In fact, husbands, if your prayers are not being answered, take into account how you are treating your wife. You promised to love her and make her happy, yet the opposite is true of you; maybe you've been a thorn in her side by not treating her well, verbally and physically abusing her every chance you get, being a source of sadness and bitterness because of your continuous infidelity, being spiteful, etc. This is the cause of your unanswered prayers! Husbands are given instructions from Yahuah in 1 Peter 3:7, "*Likewise, ye husbands, dwell with them according to knowledge, giving honour unto the wife, as unto the weaker vessel, and as being heirs together of the grace of life; that your prayers be not hindered.*"

Malachi 2:13-15 says, "*This is another thing you do. You cover Yahuah's altar with your tears. You cry and moan, because he does not accept your offerings and is not pleased with what you bring. You ask, 'Why?' It is because Yahuah sees how you treated the wife you married when you were young. You broke your promise to her, even though she was your partner and you had an agreement with her. Yahuah made husbands and wives to become one body and one spirit for his purpose – so they would have children who are true to Yahuah. So be careful, and do not break your promise to the wife you married when you were young*" (NCV). The relationship between a husband and wife is meant to be one of love, respect and support. They are there to help each other. Husbands, if you are not treating your wife right, I suggest you repent and start treating that woman right so Yahuah can answer your prayers.

Biblical Roles of Wives

The Bible asks the question: Who can find a virtuous woman? For her price is far above rubies. I believe we were given an example of what a "good wife" is in Proverbs 31:10-31 because Yahuah foresaw the power struggle and role reversal that we see in a lot of marriage these days.

The Good Wife — Her Attributes

10 It is hard to find a good wife, because she is worth more than rubies.

11 Her husband trusts her completely. With her, he has everything he needs.

12 She does him good and not harm for as long as she lives.

13 She looks for wool and flax and likes to work with her hands.

14 She is like a trader's ship, bringing food from far away.

15 She gets up while it is still dark and prepares food for her family and feeds her servant girls.

16 She inspects a field and buys it. With money she earned, she plants a vineyard.

17 She does her work with energy, and her arms are strong.

18 She knows that what she makes is good. Her lamp burns late into the night.

19 She makes thread with her hands and weaves her own cloth.

20 She welcomes the poor and helps the needy.

21 She does not worry about her family when it snows, because they all have fine clothes to keep them warm.

22 She makes coverings for herself; her clothes are made of linen and other expensive material.

23 Her husband is known at the city meetings, where he makes decisions as one of the leaders of the land.

24 She makes linen clothes and sells them and provides belts to the merchants.

25 She is strong and is respected by the people. She looks forward to the future with joy.

26 She speaks wise words and teaches others to be kind.

27 She watches over her family and never wastes her time.

28 Her children speak well of her. Her husband also praises her,

29 saying, "There are many fine women, but you are better than all of them."

30 Charm can fool you, and beauty can trick you, but a woman who respects YAHUAH should be praised.

31 Give her the reward she has earned; she should be praised in public for what she has done. (NCV)

 Let's look at some of the verses starting at verse 13, "She looks for wool, and flax, and likes to work with her hands," and along with that, verse 16, "she inspects a field and buys it. With money she earned, she plants a vineyard." And 24, "She makes linen clothes and sells them and provides belts to the merchants." What do these three verses tell us? The Proverbs 31 woman was a Stayhomepreneur, a BOSS chick; even as she was a stay-at-home mom, she took care of her family and did domestic chores (verse 15); she had her business and excelled at it. Being a stay-at-home mom does not mean you still can't pursue your own ambitions; it means you don't let your ambitions interfere in your home responsibility (which *you* willingly signed up for by getting married). I personally believe that *every* wife is supposed to be a Stayhomepreneur. When we choose to work outside of the home for someone, we limit ourselves. We walk outside of our purpose and hand the authority bestowed on our husband over to someone else, i.e. your boss will have more authority over you than your husband does as whatever your boss says goes, even if it's at the detriment of your family.

Let's Look at the Main Roles of Wives.
Helper, Supporter, Encourager — The Bible tells us in Genesis 2: 20-24, "*...but for Adam there was not found an help meet for him. And Yahuah caused a deep sleep to fall upon Adam, and he slept: and he took one of his ribs, and closed up the flesh instead thereof; and the rib, which Yahuah had taken from man, made he a woman, and brought her unto the man. And Adam said, 'This is now bone of my bones, and flesh of my flesh: she shall be called Woman, because she was taken out of Man [sic].'*" The husband is the "head" of the home and as the saying goes, "the wife is the neck." The neck supports the head; without it, the head is unable to carry out any of its functions.

Submission to Husband's Leadership — Wives are supposed to submit to their husbands' leadership. *"But as the church is subject to Christ, so also wives should be subject to their husbands in everything [respecting both their position as protector and their responsibility to Yahuah as head of the house]"* (AMP, Ephesians 5:24).

Good Witness — Yahuah tells us to marry a believer, but if we find ourselves unequally yoked in marriage, He charged us wives with the job of bringing our husbands to Christ as shown in 1 Peter 3:1-4, *"In the same way, you wives should yield to your husbands. Then, if some husbands do not obey Yahuah's teaching, they will be persuaded to believe without anyone saying a word to them. They will be persuaded by the way their wives live. Your husbands will see the pure lives you live with your respect for Yahuah. It is not fancy hair, gold jewellery or fine clothes that should make you beautiful. No, your beauty should come from within you - the beauty of a gentle and quiet spirit that will never be destroyed and is very precious to Him"* (NCV) in other words, you are the bible your spouse won't read as well as the church he won't attend. Your actions will determine if he will get to know Christ.

Child bearer, Nurturer, and Homemaker — Some women dislike hearing this because they feel it reduces them to nothing more than a meek, non-opinion-having homemaker. But look what Yahuah's Word teaches in Titus 2:5, *"To be self–controlled, chaste, home makers, good natured {kind-hearted}, adapting and* *subordinating themselves to their husbands, that Yahuah's word may not be exposed to reproach (blasphemed or discredited)"* (AMPC). The previous verses mentioned in Proverbs 31:10-31 also show that the home (taking care of the family and everything that has to do with the home) should be the woman's primary responsibility.

Just like you have husbands who mistreat their wives, there are some wives who make their husbands' lives miserable and the Bible gives us several examples: 1) Proverbs 12:4, *"A virtuous woman is a crown to her husband: but she that maketh ashamed is a rottenness in his bones,"* 2) Proverbs 25:24, *"It is better to dwell in the corner of the housetop, than with a brawling woman in a wide house,"* 3) Proverbs 21:19, *"It is better to dwell in the wilderness, than with a contentious and angry woman,"* 4) Proverbs 27:15, *"A continual dropping in a very rainy day and a contentious woman are alike."* Like I stated earlier, the relationship between a husband and wife is meant to be one of love, respect and support. If you are a wife who causes strife, I suggest you repent from the strife that could be destroying your marriage and family.

Does Yahuah View Women as Inferior to Men?

Many of Yahuah's principles concerning marriage have been received negatively by women because the scripture says woman are supposed to be submissive to men and are the "weaker" sex. NEWSFLASH — we *are* the weaker sex. Does this mean we are inferior to men? Absolutely not. But based on the role Yahuah designed and created us for, we are the weaker sex. I would as well say men are 'weak' vessels but women are 'weaker' vessels. Both sexes can't serve the same purposes, yet their individual purposes are complementary. We women are the weaker sex and until we accept the purpose Yahuah created us for, we cannot live the true life He purposed us for and we miss the rewards that come with living according to His will. Embracing our womanhood and femininity does equate to being gentle and agreeable but that does not make us fragile or frail.

I personally believe Yahuah holds us wives in higher esteem than the men which is why He gives a reward to the man who finds a wife, as written in Proverbs 18: 22, *"Whoso findeth a wife findeth a good thing, and obtaineth Yahuah's favour."* There is no Scripture that gives wives blessings for having a husband/getting married. Many women, myself included, are quick to quote that Scripture but it begs the question: are we really a wife as described in the Scripture? Are we submissive and respectful like Yahuah says we should be? Are we being a wife according to His will, or are we a wife according to our own will and standards?

I've come to understand that submission as Yahuah intended means nothing more than being sensitive to our husband's needs and being respectful of his leadership as the "head" of the household. His job is to go out and make the bacon, love and take care of his wife, children and household. Too often, women have made it easy on men by taking the provider role and excelling in it. In doing this, however, they inadvertently added to their own responsibility of maintaining their husband, children and household, as the husbands didn't pick up those responsibilities like the women did. The husbands still expect the home front to be taken care of even while you help out with their own role, but can you blame them? They never asked the women to take over—women just did. We were made as the support for our husband and not the other way round. We've lost our focus because our focus is elsewhere, on our career and work (outside of the home for someone else) and it's killing our marriages. While Yahuah is not against wives working, He doesn't want us in the provider role because it goes against His plan for marriages. Our work should not interfere or prevent us from carrying out our responsibilities to our husbands and children. I believe the question we need to start asking ourselves is, are we able to work outside of the home and still give a 100% commitment to our husband, children and home responsibilities? I don't believe so (at least in my opinion anyway).

Principles for Both Husband and Wife

Sexual Relations: Yahuah's Word is clear about sexual relations between a man and a woman. In 1 Corinthians 7: 2, we read, *"Nevertheless, because of sexual immorality, let each man have his own wife and let each woman have her own husband. Let the husband render to his wife the affection due her, and likewise also the wife to her* *husband. The wife does not have authority over her own body, but the husband does. And likewise the husband does not have authority over his own body, but the wife does. Do not deprive one another except with consent for a time that you may give yourselves to fasting and prayer; and come together again so that Satan does not tempt you because of your lack of self-control"* (NKJV).   Really? So all the, "I'm tired," "I have a headache," and other excuses we women are notorious for are "wrong." This Scripture tells us that husbands and wives need to consider one another's sexual needs. We need to know that our bodies belong to one another and we cannot withhold sex just because we don't feel like it. Hebrews 13:4 says, *"Marriage is honourable in all, and the bed undefiled; but whoremongers [a person who has dealings with prostitutes, especially a sexually promiscuous man] and adulterers Yahuah will judge."* So based on this scripture, as long as you're not bringing a third party (person, animal or thing) into your bed, you are good. I've heard some people say oral sex is wrong. I may be wrong but *my belief* is that it is wrong only if you are fornicating; if you are married and are having oral sex especially on your bed, your bed is undefiled. (Corny joke, I know) but in all seriousness, I believe whatever a married couple does, as long as it's between the both of them, no third party, no foreign objects being inserted into their bodies; then their bed is undefiled, so anything and everything goes.

Is Divorce Allowed in Yahuah's Kingdom?

Does Yahuah allow divorce? The scripture tells us He hates divorce. Malachi 2:16 says, "For I hate divorce," Says *Yahuah,* *"and him who covers his garment with wrong and violence," says* *Yahuah. "Therefore keep watch on your spirit, so that you do not deal* *treacherously [with your wife]"* (AMP).

Yeshua went on to tell us more about divorce when asked about it in Mark 10:3-12, *"Yeshua answered, '**What did** **Moses command you to do?**' They said, 'Moses allowed a man to* *write out divorce papers and send her away.' Yeshua said, 'Moses* *wrote that command for you because you were stubborn. But when* *Yahuah made the world, 'he made them male and female.' 'So a man* *will leave his father and mother and be united with his wife, and the* *two will become one body. So there are not two, but one. Yahuah has* *joined the two together, so no one should separate them.'* Later, in the house, his followers asked Yeshua again about the question of divorce. He answered, *'Anyone who divorces his wife and marries* *another woman is guilty of adultery against her. And the woman who* *divorces her husband and marries another man is guilty of* *adultery.'"*{NCV} The corresponding passage in Matthew 19: 9 says, *"And I say unto you, whosoever shall put away his wife, except* *it be for fornication and shall marry another, committed adultery: and* *whoso marrieth her which is put away doth commit adultery.'"* This shows us that the *only* grounds for divorce is found in a situation of sexual immorality where either spouse is having sexual relations with another man/woman. They can divorce one another but because they are already married and their souls tied, no remarriage is permitted. Romans 7:3 also tell us, *"So while her husband is alive, she would be committing adultery if she married another man. But if her husband dies, she is free from that law and does not commit adultery when/if she remarries"* (NLT).

Chapter 17

Other Marriage Matters

Many people spend more time in planning the wedding than they do in planning the marriage ~ Zig Ziglar

The Purpose of Engagement

I had always wondered why more men than women got cold feet and called off weddings, or left someone at the altar. With what I know now about marriage from Yahuah's perspective, I believe it's because **some** men, realised they are not up to the task or perhaps think of everything that could potentially go wrong in the marriage, so they end up pulling out. In the meantime, many engaged women, myself included, have our heads in the clouds, dreaming about how marvellous the wedding will be from the day we get engaged, instead of thinking of the actual marriage and how to prepare for it.

The truth of the matter is that many of us women want to be brides but not wives. We want the wedding but not the actual marriage as we still want to be independent and bring a feminist approach to marriage. Marriage was created by Yahuah and if we choose to go into it, we have to 'play' by the rules He's set. We can't pick and choose what we want and don't want when it comes to the principles of marriage. If you don't want to be submissive and respectful as a wife or love your wife unconditionally as a husband, then don't get married. Don't get married and then try to change the "rules" of marriage and still expect Yahuah to bless your union. This is why there is a courting period i.e. the engagement period wherein you get to know each other and share your vision.

The purpose of the engagement period is to find out the most important thing – are we sure this is the person we want to make the commitment of being married to forever? Too many of us are "blinded" during the dating phase. Engagement is the time to prepare for the marriage journey ahead of us and to start practicing the different roles Yahuah has for us as husbands and wives. We hear a lot of people say "you shouldn't lose yourself when you get married," but in reality, we are supposed to shed our individual selves. We are supposed to leave those behind in the old chapter (singlehood) in order to become one with our spouses in this new chapter of our lives but we totally miss the purpose of this period and go into marriage blind and unprepared.

It wasn't until I started writing this book (two and a half years into marriage) that the "scales fell off my eyes." I realised how wrong I had been in my approach to marriage. Knowing what I know now, I can't honestly say I would have jumped into marriage when I did because I went in for all the wrong reasons. Nevertheless, there is nobody on the face of the earth I would love to go through this journey with other than my Mr. Wonderful. While it's still a challenge to be a wife as Yahuah intended, I am learning and it's a humbling process which I believe every wife needs to learn. Even if you make all the money in the world, give your husband the opportunity to be the head of the home as well as provider for you. In my case, I really didn't have a choice; I went from being Ms. Independent with a great career as a Real Estate agent to a stay-at-home mom relying on my husband for pretty much everything. But that did a lot for our relationship. I got to see and experience my husband as the provider, and he never made me feel inadequate because he was providing for me. I know this is a big issue for women these days because they don't want to rely on a man in case he screws them over. I totally get it but I believe that depends on the type of man you are married to as my experience was different; my husband became my Knight in Shining Armour. The things I could no longer do or provide for myself, he had an opportunity to do for me and that made my respect for him grow. He's done an excellent job of being a leader, protector, provider, lover, friend and life mate, so I don't mind being the wife who belongs at home, in the kitchen, in the living room and in the other room (even though I now run a Spiritual "Life" Coach business, shameless plug). He's worth every minute of being in those rooms. My prayer is that we all go into marriage for the right reasons, knowing the true purpose of marriage and embracing our roles as specified by Yahuah so that our marriage will edify Him and create Kingdom Ambassador Children.

***

Modern-Day Feminism in Marriage

We hear a great deal about feminism and women's rights these days and quite frankly, it's starting to work my nerves. My thing with feminism is this: "it's lost the plot;" these modern-day *feministas* have taken it a bit off track. Feminism started as a movement aimed at equal rights for women who were oppressed as its purpose focused on overturning legal inequalities, particularly women's suffrage (right to vote). Feminism also broadened the debate to include cultural inequalities, gender norms, and the role of women in society. I understand there are some countries who still need this mode of feminism to get these rights I listed above, but I'm not referring to those women. I'm referring to wives who practice this evolved form of feminism which pretty much boils down to competing with their husbands. The key words we need to focus on here are **women** and **oppressed.** 1)

All wives are women but not all women are wives. Again, this is talking to wives, not all women. 2) There is no oppression in marriage; or should I say there shouldn't be oppression in marriage. If there is, then you probably married someone you didn't 'know' long enough.

I may be wrong, but I don't believe people change drastically from one extreme to the other. One doesn't all of a sudden become a cheat, wife/husband beater, paedophile, rapist, etc. While these qualities may be repressed when you just meet, as soon as they start getting comfortable with you, their real selves will become evident in some things they do. When most people meet someone new, they present a "representative" of themselves who will "put up an act" to be the person most people want, i.e. loving, charming, sweet, friendly, attentive, happy, etc. But soon enough, red flags which I like to refer to as "the true self" will start to emerge. The person may become hype for no real reason and go from 0-60, they may become controlling or uncompromising, they may start cheating/sleeping around, and they may hit you and try to make up by giving you things. Whatever the case may be, they start to show signs of their "true selves" because like the saying goes, "The soul has no secret that the behaviour does not reveal." The only way a person will carry on an act for a long time is if the person is a socio/psychopath and I want to believe most people aren't. If we pay attention to people's behaviours and wait before jumping into marriage, we will know the "real" person and can then decide if they are someone we want to be with so we don't face oppression in marriage. Now, If it turns out you really did marry an "actor or a psychopath," in other words, someone who sold you fake goods, and you find yourself in a marriage you ordinarily would not have signed up for, I suggest you pray about it and let the Holy Spirit guide you. However, don't stop there. You need to talk to your spouse and see if there are things you can both do to make your relationship better. For example, you can do the Love Dare challenge (thelovedarebook.com). Sometimes, one person's effort can change the dynamics of a marriage and that effort encourages the uncooperative spouse to join the process of saving the marriage and being a better spouse. Maybe you can go to counselling, talk to your pastor, or other Bible mentors. Of course, this is assuming there is no form of abuse going on, if there is, **separate** immediately. I say separate because I believe people can be healed, but ultimately, it is your marriage and only you know what the situation is.

***

Feminism allowed women's voices that had been silenced for years to be heard. Women started saying, "Hey, it's not just a man's world. It's also a woman's world and our opinions and experiences matter too so take that into consideration when making laws that affect us." But feminism has evolved into something completely different. I believe in Yahuah's order, so I believe the man is the head. Adam (man) was the one Yahuah created to "rule" this earth, so He formed Adam based on the characteristics and skills he needed to do the "job." Eve (Woman) came in on a different purpose, not to rule the earth but to love the man and to take care of him, as well as the children and home. Yahuah created her based on what she needed to accomplish those goals.

Feminism has gone from trying to get our voices heard and taking our struggles into consideration, too, to doing a whole lot of competing (trying to rule the earth) and not a lot of loving (our purpose whether you agree or not). We already know we are better than men in a lot of things (sorry men), so why bother proving it to them? How about we focus on exactly what Yahuah put us on this earth for and go back to **order** and see if our lives don't get better? We need to let go of modern-day feminism **in marriage because** like oil and water, they don't mix.

With all that said, I can't get off this topic without saying something to the men. 1 Corinthians 11:3 says, *"But I would have you know, that the head of every man is Christ; and the head of the woman is the man; and the head of Christ is Yahuah."* Many men want the woman to uphold the Bible principles of being a submissive and respectful wife, but the men don't want to do their part which is, submit to Christ's leadership, be loving, faithful, be the provider, protector, etc. as Yahuah laid them out. It doesn't work that way. It's challenging for a woman especially one that's a follower of Christ to submit to a man who's not submitting to Christ. You can't eat your cake and have it, too. Then we have the men that have gone wimpy and soft. They've let their wives clip their cajones and turn them into house husbands. Then they wonder why she's just not that into them anymore? Psst! Come closer; let me let you in on a little secret: she doesn't find you manly anymore (and don't bother asking her; she's going to tell you I don't know what I'm talking about). What she finds attractive are the men at her workplace, the men she sees grinding, being about their J.O.B day in day out. That's a turn on! You see, we women are funny creatures, we want a man that will *help* us with the cooking and cleaning but not one that stays home and does it as a "day job;" that's not sexy to us. What's sexy is a husband cooking dinner for his wife after he's gone out to make the bacon. Sexy is when a man comes home from work and still helps with the children and house chores. Of course, I can't negate the fact that being a Stay-at-Home Dad is a wonderful and an honourable thing to do, but I also can't deny the fact that it's not what the order of marriage should be. Let me say it again, it's not sexy! You want to keep your wife interested just as she should keep you interested; being a stay-at-home dad is not one of the ways to do it. No woman in her right mind (in my opinion) would want to see her husband in that role day in day out.

Husband and wives, it's time to claim your roles back. Make a decision to have a biblical marriage and marry only a spouse who wants the same things. If both parties set their expectations before getting married, they can make a decision on whether to get married or not if those expectations are not being met during the engagement period. If your expectations are not being met during the engagement, DO NOT GET MARRIED to him or her and wait for the person Yahuah ordained you for.

It's time for us to stop treating our marriages like child's play and embrace the real and true purpose of marriage. Come in prepared for battle, because that's what it is; there is a battle set by the devil to conquer all marriages and destroy families (especially biblical ones) so come in to marriage ready to work your behinds off with the understanding that no matter what hurtful and devastating circumstances may happen during the course of your marriage, you will come out of it together as one, as DIVORCE IS NOT AN OPTION because if it's an option, you will take it! Easier said than done, I know, but it can be done. We've got to start choosing our marriages and not just keep giving it away without putting up a fight, like the devil wants.

To my divorced couples, as long as you're still single, i.e. not married to anyone, this is a call to action for you to get back with your ex-spouse (as long as there was no sort of abuse or maltreatment). Take a stand to get your marriage back on track, and let's start getting and staying married for better and for worse. Please, people! Let's get this broken marriage epidemic under repair.

Relationship Tips

Make Christ the bedrock of your marriage.
The principles we live by will determine how we handle decisions/conflicts in our relationships. When we consider the teachings of Christ before we make any decisions we **will** always do the right thing even when we want to do otherwise.

Do not jump into marriage.
This does not mean the marriage will be perfect, but you will have time to gauge the compatibility of you and your partner's characteristics and personalities as well as see each other's "ugly phases" of emotions and know whether it's something you want to deal with for the rest of your lives.

Be equally yoked.
You may have heard this saying before about being equally yoked which comes from 2 Corinthians 6:14: *"Do not be unequally yoked together with unbelievers. For what fellowship has righteousness with lawlessness? And what communion has light with darkness?"* (NKJV). This one is a biggie! It means that a believer and follower of Christ should marry the same, a believer. While this saying is commonly used when referring to romantic relationships between a believer and unbeliever, in context, 2 Corinthians 6:14 is referring to every type of association whether it is a friendship, a romantic or business relationship. I do, however, concur on the emphasis on romantic relationships,

especially marriage. The Bible tells us that when two people marry, the two shall become one flesh so a believer marrying an unbeliever is two people with opposing beliefs coming together which will make the marriage relationship challenging. Although Scripture was referring to believers not being yoked to unbelievers, it goes further than that because even unbelievers can still be unequally yoked since we all have different beliefs, values, cultures and priorities. I suggest before getting into marriage, you make sure that you both are on the same page; you both want the same things and are working towards the same goal (whatever that goal is for your marriage). Marrying someone with different beliefs, values and or priorities can have severe negative consequences when the "honeymoon" phase is over and you get hit with the reality of the situation. Choose your partner wisely.

Expectations/Acceptance

Because he asked you to marry him, does not necessarily mean he is ready to be committed and monogamous. If he is, this will be apparent during the engagement period. Most of us assume our significant others will make those "good changes" because that's what people are supposed to do when they get married. Sometimes we may not express our expectations, and then we start to get frustrated when changes don't happen after the wedding. I say, make sure the changes you expect to happen once you're married are happening during the engagement period. If they're not, you have to choose whether this is something you are willing to live with. If you go into that marriage accepting the "bad behaviours," what you have done is enabled them and trust me, they recognise that fact and will not change — you've agreed to accept whatever circumstance and bad behaviour rear up during the course of your marriage. Acceptance is key and that may mean accepting that the person you are engaged/married to isn't serious about changing. The ring and wedding were just to show you they love you, but they have no plans on changing. I always say, make your decision of being with someone on the present and never on the future.

Marry Your Friend, as well as Your Lover
Make sure you and your husband/wife are friends first and like each other before you jump into a relationship. Most of us see a guy or girl and are attracted to them because of the way they look, the way they dress, where they live, what they drive or what they have, and go into relationships for those reasons. Even when we see something we don't like, we are consumed by what we do like so we don't really give what we don't like that much thought. Once the novelty of the relationship wears off and we start to notice those things we should have paid attention to in the beginning, we claim the person changed. No, honey, he/she was always like that but we just chose to ignore those things because we were caught up in what we wanted to see. The saying, "There's a thin line between love and hate" is not just a movie; it's a reality. Once the butterflies in the tummy have flown away (and trust me, they will) and your heart now

skips not from love but more from he/she gets on my nerves, what will sustain your relationship is the friendship and the likeness you have for one another. If there's no friendship, the relationship will not stand the test of time. Your friendship and likeness for one another will help you choose to love each other in those moments when you don't really feel the love because as we all know; love is a choice, not a feeling.

Food for thought: Like Reverend Ejibe Eme Ogonna asks, "If Yahuah needed people to show unbelievers a good example of marriage, would He be able to send them to your house and use your marriage as an example?"

PS: WOMEN, femininity is sexy. Let's hone it!

Chapter 18

Children

Train a child in the way he should go and when he is old, he will not depart from it~ Proverbs 22:6

Yahuah blesses us with children as a blessing and reward. In Psalm 127:3, we read, *"Lo, children are an heritage of Yahuah: and the fruit of the womb is his reward [sic]."* Yahuah gives us children so that we may raise them to become Ambassadors that will advance His Kingdom. Children are born with "blank slates" and are pretty much like video cameras with legs—they "record" everything they experience on their slates. Most of us have heard the saying, "Do as I say, not as I do," but we forget that the children of today turn out to be adults of tomorrow and will most likely gravitate towards something he/she has experienced rather than what he/she is being or has been told to do. If a child grew up seeing a parent being promiscuous, an alcoholic, druggie, having children out of wedlock, in a broken home, etc., no matter how much you may talk to that child about not going down the same path, nine times out of ten, the child will go down that same path because that's the path he/she is familiar with, it will take everything in them to fight to go down a totally different path that they are not familiar with.

We parents owe it to our children to be great examples for them and that starts with giving them a *loving* two-parent household to grow up in. In the beautiful words of Isaac Kubvoruno, "Children are wonderful gifts from Yahuah but children are a temporary assignment entrusted to our care for a season. Never let your children run or ruin your marriage. Yes, children are important and we are commanded to raise them in the fear of Yahuah but they should not be the epicentre of marriage. Marriage is the partnership of husband, wife and Yahuah and children are the fruit. Fruit is seasonal but the marriage tree exists before, during and after the fruit is gone. Some people make the mistake of prioritizing children above their spouses. Children are not the glue that binds couples together, Yahuah is. If your marriage is held together by the children, one wonders what will happen when the children are gone. Ensure that your marriage lasts after your children are gone by spending time building your marriage while your children are still there." In other words, do not put your children above your spouse. You are one with your spouse and your spouse's needs come first. This is in no way saying you should neglect your children—far from it. But if the parental relationship is not top priority, the children will not be okay.

What's in a Name?

A name can either be a gift or a curse. A name can empower or cripple us and it can determine the course of a child's life. Most of us have heard about the prayer of Jabez, which is usually referenced when the topic of prosperity comes up, but the prayer has little to do with prosperity and everything to do with his name. 1 Chronicles 4:9 says, "*And Jabez was more honourable than his brethren: and his mother called his name Jabez, saying 'Because I bare him with sorrow.' And Jabez called on Yahuah saying. 'Oh, that thou wouldest bless me indeed, and enlarge my coast, and that thine hand might be with me, and that you wouldest keep me from evil, that it may not grieve me!' And Yahuah granted him that which he requested.*"

The purpose of Jabez's prayer was for Yahuah to lift the curse off his life and live free from the sorrow his mother bestowed upon him when she named him. Jabez's mother named him based on the sorrowful circumstances surrounding his birth. We can see from his prayer this name was stifling him. If Yahuah hadn't answered his prayer, he was destined to cause pain to people and he wanted that changed. He prayed to Yahuah to bless him and enlarge his territory i.e. release him from the limited life his mother "cursed" him with, to be with him throughout the course of his life, and to keep him from evil and for him not to bring pain to people. Why would he pray for him not to cause pain? Because that's what his mother bestowed upon him. The last thing we read is that Yahuah granted his request, which means Jabez's prayer defeated the curse that was his name.

"The Bible goes on to show that Yahuah also took it upon Himself to change people's names if their names didn't match the assignment He had given them. He changed Abram's "high father" name to "Abraham, father of a multitude" (Genesis 17:5), and his wife's name from "Sarai, my princess," to "Sarah, mother of nations" (Genesis 17:15). He changed Jacob's "supplanter" name to "Israel, having power with Yahuah" (Genesis 32:28). He changed Simon's "Yahuah has heard" name to "Peter, rock" (John 1:42). Why did Yeshua occasionally call Peter "Simon" after He had changed His name to "Peter"? Probably because Simon sometimes acted like his old self instead of the rock Yahuah called him to be. The same is true for Jacob. Yahuah continued to call him "Jacob" to remind him of his past and to remind him to depend on Yahuah's strength. Why did Yahuah choose new names for some people? The Bible doesn't give us His reasons, but perhaps it was to let them know they were destined for a new mission in life. The new name was a way to let them in on the divine plan and also to assure them that Yahuah's plan would be fulfilled in them."

(Culled from *Bible Answers for Almost All Your Questions* by Elmer Towns and *Logos Bible Software*).

Leaving out the biblical aspect, plenty of research suggests the name chosen impacts a child's life well into adulthood. With all that said, it is our responsibility as guardians of these children to give them names that will build them up, rather than naming them after a fruit, colour, weather, destination, direction, where we are going, how we are feeling, what we are drinking, eating or driving.

Useful Things to Teach Our Children

• Teach children to meditate on Yahuah's words day and night as instructed in Joshua 1:8, "*This book of the law shall not depart out of thy mouth; but thou shalt meditate therein day and night, that thou mayest observe to do accordingly to all that is written therein; for then thou shalt make thy way prosperous, and then thou shalt have good success.*"

• Teach children the difference between temporary defeat and failure and show them how to search for the silver lining in all situations.

• Teach children to express their own thoughts fearlessly and to accept or reject at will all ideas of others, reserving to themselves the privilege of always relying upon their own judgment.

• Teach children to be definite in all things, beginning with the choice of a definite major purpose in life.

- Teach children what to eat, how much to eat, and what the relationship between proper eating and sound health is.
- Teach children the nature and the value of self-control.
- Teach children the true nature of the golden rule and above all, show them the operation of this principle: Everything they do to and for another, they also do to and for themselves.
- Teach children not to have opinions unless they are formed from facts or beliefs, which may reasonably be accepted as facts.
- Teach children that cigarettes, liquor, narcotics and over-indulgence in sex destroy the power of will and lead to the habit of drifting. Do not just forbid these evils; explain them so your kids will know why.
- Teach children the danger of believing anything merely because their parents, religious instructors or someone else says it is so.
- Teach children that their only real limitations are those that they set up or permit others to establish in their own minds.
- Teach them that man can achieve whatever man can conceive and believe.
- Teach children that *"the rich ruleth over the poor, and the borrower is servant to the lender."* In other words, borrowing/debt is bad and the borrower is slave to the lender (Proverbs 22:7).
- Teach children to be true to themselves at all times and since they cannot please everybody, therefore, they need to do a

good job of pleasing themselves. (Culled from *Outwitting the Devil* by Napoleon Hill).

Protecting Our Children

I debated long and hard whether this chapter of my life should go in this book and the dominating winner was a resounding NO! But I have this crazy idea that my purpose is bigger than me and the chapters of my life. While I know including the following story opens me up to peoples' opinions and judgments, denying these experiences will be denying who I am and the experiences that have helped shape me into the woman I have become. Plus, it is time to speak up, so we can prevent other innocent children from getting tainted. Once children are violated, most of them will repeat the cycle. Whether in a playful or abusive way, the abuse will likely be repeated. If we can prevent it from happening, we can STOP the cycle.

Growing up, I thought it "normal" for all women to have an affinity to other women. I would have even bet my life on it. Later in life as an adult, I was at one point part of a marriage group on Facebook and one day, someone posted a question asking if it was normal for women to be attracted to other women. I was so sure a lot of women would answer "yes," so imagine my surprise when it wasn't so. Several women responded with it not being normal because they had never been attracted to another woman. I couldn't believe it. How could that be? I mean it was socially acceptable. Katy Perry even sang about kissing a girl and liking it and the song was a yuge hit (in Trump's voice), so it had to be true, right? Someone else, who I guess was in the same boat as me, replied with a comment, that **most** people who have an affinity towards the same sex are that way because they were in some sort of a sexual situation with the person of the same sex when they were younger. She polled that question and to everyone's amazement, it was true. All the people that responded to that question had been in one way or the other involved with the same sex sexually, and that was when all my memories came flooding back.

When I was between the ages of six and seven and living in Eric Moore Towers, there was a field of grass behind our building, and most of us children loved to play in that field. I remember being taken there frequently by an older female friend (who happened to be a maid to one of the families that lived there), and we would play the game "mummy and daddy." In the course of playing, she would kiss and touch me inappropriately and tell me I was her special friend. The family must have eventually moved away because I stopped seeing her. I remember by the time I was ten, I introduced one of my female friends to the game. We played it a handful of times, but shortly after that, it started feeling wrong (probably because I had stopped thinking boys had cooties and had become googly-eyed for them). We stopped playing the game and I somehow buried that memory.

Remembering my past and reading the comments on Facebook were life-changing times. Life as I knew it changed for me because I felt damaged. I realised the occasional attraction I had to some women was not normal; it stemmed from "playing mummy and daddy (this is why it's important to teach kids at an early age about sexually play behaviour). I felt violated and put in a position I didn't want to be in because I never got the chance to choose whether I wanted to play like that or not. I started to get angry, and then it dawned on me that the maid was probably a victim that continued the cycle (most people are), and since I was the one that introduced the game to my friend, my friend could feel the same way I was feeling. That anger quickly turned to guilt, sympathy, remorse, embarrassment—you name it—but rather than let those emotions consume me, I asked for forgiveness from Yahuah. I immediately started searching Facebook for my childhood friend so I could apologise to her but couldn't find her. Most importantly, however, I forgave myself so that I wouldn't wallow in those negative emotions. It then dawned on me that the occasional attraction to women would be my burden to carry because as we all know, it is a sin.

Sexual Assault/Molestation
I was about sixteen years old the time I was molested by a family friend; I woke up to him on top of me with his hand covering my mouth in case I tried to scream. I could feel his hand all over me and I cringed with every touch. He told me he didn't want to rape me because that's not what he was about, but he would if he had to. He told me he was going to take his

hand off my mouth and I shouldn't scream and if I did, he would tell whoever came that I invited him into my bed. I thought of screaming but I was afraid of what would happen if I did and nobody believed me and believed him instead, so I let it happen. It was kind of an unwritten rule of: "I will have sex with you whenever I want but I won't force myself on you or even rape you but you can't say no." He would buy me gifts and call me his girlfriend in front of everyone and everyone thought it was just a joke and laughed it off; in his sick, twisted and perverted mind, I truly believe he did. He would tell me he wasn't doing anything wrong because I was already having sex (which I was), and he knew I wanted him because he saw the way I looked at him.

Of course, I never wanted to have sex with him but I started believing I was giving him a look and that's what made him want to have sex with me. I was angry with myself because this was not what I wanted but I felt I had no choice. I didn't think I could tell anyone because I felt they would either not believe me or blame me for it happening to me. I started feeling guilty that it was my fault he picked me because if I hadn't given him the flirting look he said I did and I wasn't already having sex, I wouldn't be in this predicament. His job transferred him out of the country and he moved to London. I was glad when it stopped and somehow buried that experience deep inside me.

I was in London in May of 2011 for a conference when I ran into him. All the memories and feelings of hurt, anger and guilt hit me like a ton of bricks. He, however, acted like everything was okay; he even had the nerve to show me a picture of his wife and two beautiful children. I was waiting for his apology, but it never came. I didn't even know when I blurted out, "I forgive you."

He chuckled and said, "What for?"

I said, "Having sex with me even when I didn't want to."

He looked stunned and said, "But you wanted it."

I was taken aback and asked, "You really believe that, don't you?"

He answered, "Yes."

I told him contrary to what he believed, I never once wanted him. Yes, I was having sex then, but it was with my boyfriend who I chose and agreed to have sex with. I told him he took away my right to choose whom I wanted to have sex with. He looked shocked and said he was sorry, but those words did nothing for me. I had longed to hear those words during the time he used to have his way with me because I thought it would make me feel better, but hearing his apology now did absolutely nothing for me.

I took a deep breath, looked him right in the eye, and told him I forgave him. I instantly felt this weight which I didn't even know I was carrying lifted off my shoulders. That was when I realised I never really needed his apology. All I needed to do was forgive myself and know that it was nothing I did that made him choose me. He chose me because my family life was dysfunctional, and it helped his cause.

***

I believe Nigerian kids as well as other African kids are more susceptible to abuse because they are around more help staff e.g. drivers, house helps, washer men, mechanics, carpenters, etc. We need to start by educating the children and parents around us about what is and what's not acceptable especially, while playing. "Our Body Safety Rules" written by Sandy k. Wurtele, Ph.D, and Feather Berkower, MSW is a great place to start.

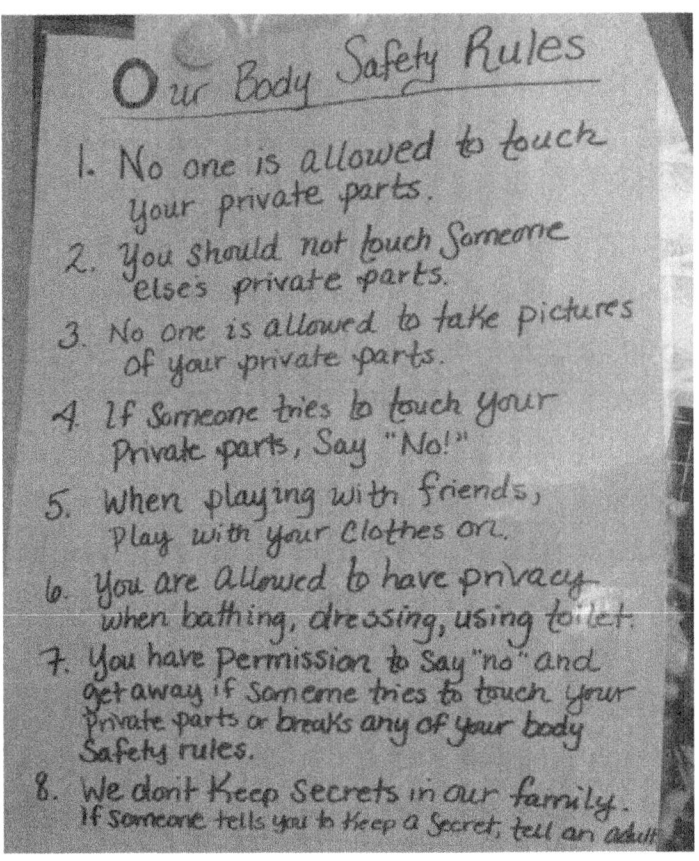

Let's always remember that Yahuah bestowed us with children, not for us to mould into little mini-me's, but for us to protect and help bring out the potential and purpose Yahuah put them on this earth for.

In Kahlil Gibran's famous words:

Your children are not your children.

They are the sons and daughters of Life's longing for itself.

They come through you but not from you, and though they are with you, yet they belong not to you.

You may give them your love but not your thoughts, for they have their own thoughts. You may house their bodies but not their souls, for their souls dwell in the house of tomorrow, which you cannot visit, not even in your dreams.

You may strive to be like them, but seek not to make them like you,

For life goes not backward nor tarries with yesterday.

Chapter 19

Dead Things

Let food be thy medicine and medicine be thy food
~ Hippocrates

F ood: "Any **nutritious** substance that people or animals eat or drink, or plants absorbed in order to maintain life and growth." Just like everything Yahuah made, food was made for a purpose and that purpose is to fuel our bodies and help our growth but like many things in life, we have missed the purpose of it. Most of us eat food because it tastes good and provides a sensual pleasure for the palate.

While writing this book, the meaning of a dream I had when I was pregnant about certain sea foods was revealed to me. I didn't know what the dream meant back then because the foods in the dream were everyday foods for me. In the dream, I was back in my childhood environment Eric Moore Towers, Block C, to be exact. When I got to the entrance, I saw on the floor big and plump crabs, snails, shrimps, mussels, oysters and clams, all my favourite foods; they were already clean and ready to cook. On the floor next to them was a blue plastic basin for whoever was going to pick them up. Thinking, *ma koja mi olugbala* (this opportunity won't pass me by), I grabbed the basin and was about to start picking them up when some random guy showed up and told me not to touch them as they weren't for me. I dropped the basin, vexed that I lost out on an opportunity to get free seafood and then I woke up. In true Naija fashion, I started praying because I thought someone was trying to jazz me and possibly harm my baby by trying to feed me in the dream. I never quite forgot the dream and with all the *wahala* (trouble) I had after delivery, I was also 100% sure I was spared because I didn't touch or pick up, cook and eat all that seafood from my dream.

Fast-forward several months later, I was in the bathroom flossing when I felt the Holy Spirit say to me, "*You're eating dead things. Yahuah cannot do new things in your life, if you keep eating dead things.*" I didn't understand what that meant, and I started racking my brain to see if I could figure out what the Holy Spirit was talking about. My nail biting habit popped in my head (gross, I know) since nails are made of keratin (a protein made of dead cells). *That's got to be it*, I thought. I immediately made a decision to stop biting my nails, but I wasn't at peace. No matter how much I tried to convince myself that my nail biting had to be what the Holy Spirit had been referring to, I knew it wasn't and I continued to pray to Yahuah to reveal what He meant.

A few days later, the hubs and I were watching a movie when he showed me a cluster of something stuck to a pier. I had never seen anything like that before so I asked what it was.

He said, "Mussels."

I said, "What? The mussels we eat?"

He responded, "Yeah, didn't you know that's how mussels cluster together?" I thought, *No wonder I sometimes feel sand when eating them.*

He continued (referring to mussels and other shell fish) "Because restaurants class certain foods as a delicacy and aphrodisiac doesn't mean they are not nasty. They are all bottom feeders."

When he said that, the dream about seafood immediately flashed in my mind, but I didn't understand why. I told Abayomi I was going to stop eating mussels.

He asked why and I said, "Because they look nasty."

He said, "Really, because of that? If you see the conditions of most of the foods we eat, you would stop eating a lot of things." But my mind was already made up—no more mussels for me.

A few weeks later, I was reading the Bible and was led to read *Leviticus 11* which defines the birds, land animals, and sea creatures that are clean and unclean. Here are a few of them but for a more comprehensive list, I suggest you read it for yourself at your leisure.

Clean animals:
Land animals that chew the cud and have a divided hoof, such as cattle, deer, goats, buffalo, antelope, elk and sheep; seafood with both fins and scales, such as salmon, trout, tuna, red snapper, bass, cod, etc.; certain birds, including chickens, doves, turkey, pheasant, quail, goose, grouse; and even some insects, such as beetle, grasshoppers and locusts.

Unclean animals:
Land animals that either do not chew the cud or do not have a split hoof, such as camel, rabbit, hare, swine, dogs, cats, horses, donkeys; seafood lacking either fins or scales, such as shellfish, lobster, oysters, swordfish and catfish; some birds, such as eagles, owls, hawks, swan, pelican, stork, bats and vultures; and other creeping things that creep upon the earth; the weasel, mouse, tortoise, ferret, chameleon, lizard, snail and the mole.

Wait, what? The pig isn't the only animal we aren't supposed to eat? Some seafood too? The dream popped into my mind and very vividly, and while I don't know if this was real or imagined, I heard a "ding, ding, ding" go off in my head and the Holy Spirit saying, "Now you're catching on." These seafood and other land animals I had been eating are "dead things." How was it possible that I had never heard of this "list" before? I heard the Holy Spirit say, "Because you let other people tell you about Yahuah's Word instead of reading and experiencing it for yourself." I didn't have a response to that because that was true. Before I started writing this book, I hardly touched the Bible and sure didn't read it very much. I had heard that Yeshua had made the unclean animals clean. I brought that to the Holy Spirit and was led to read Matthew 15:1-11, specifically verses 1 and 11, "*Then some Pharisees and teachers of the law came to Jesus from Jerusalem. They asked him, why don't your followers obey the unwritten laws which have been handed down to us? They don't wash their hands before they eat. Yeshua answered, '...**Not that which goeth into the mouth defileth a man**; but that which cometh out of the mouth, this defileth a man.'*" (emphasis mine).

Another Scripture reference is Mark 7: 1-23 specifically verses 18-19, "*And he saith unto them, 'Are ye so without understanding also? Do ye not perceive, that whatsoever thing from without entereth into the man, it cannot defile him; because it entereth not into his heart, but into the belly, and goeth out into the draught, purging all meats?'*" Purging as defined by dictionary.com is to clear or empty the bowels by evacuation. And evacuation is defined as discharge, as of waste matter through the excretory passages, especially from the bowels.

In response to the question asked about eating with unwashed hands, Yeshua was saying unwashed hands do not defile man because the food will not enter into the heart but into the belly, and eventually (for the lack of a better word) will be pooped out. It says absolutely nothing about Yeshua declaring all foods clean. If you read the above verses in any other Bibles aside from the KJV and NKJV Bible version, these have been changed to include, "By saying this, he declared that every kind of food is acceptable in Yahuah's eyes" which Yeshua never said. Some people also cite Acts 10: 9-16 to support the idea that Yeshua changed the law concerning clean or unclean foods. They especially refer to verse 15, which says, *"What Yahuah hath cleansed, you must not call common."*

Acts 10: 9-16 reads, *"On the morrow, as they went on their journey, and drew nigh unto the city, Peter went up upon the housetop to pray about the sixth hour: and he became very hungry, and would have eaten: but while they made ready, he fell into a trance, and saw heaven opened, and a certain vessel descending upon him, as it had been a great sheet knit at the four corners, and let down to the earth: wherein were all manner of four-footed beasts of the earth, and wild beasts, and creeping things, and fowls of the air. And there came a voice to him, 'Rise, Peter; kill, and eat.' But Peter said, 'Not so, Yahuah; for I have never eaten anything that is common or unclean.' And the voice spake unto him again the second time, 'What Yahuah hath cleansed, that call not thou common.' This was done thrice: and the vessel was received up again into heaven."*

Now let's go back and put things in context. Let's look at what was happening before Peter sees the vision.
In Acts 10:1-8, we read, *"There was a certain man in Caesarea called Cornelius, a centurion of the band called the Italian band, a devout man, and one that feared Yahuah with all his house, which gave much alms to the people, and prayed to Yahuah always. He saw in a vision*

evidently about the ninth hour of the day an angel of Yahuah coming in to him, and saying unto him, Cornelius. And when he looked on him, he was afraid, and said, 'What is it, Yahuah? And he said unto him, 'Thy prayers and thine alms are come up for a memorial before Me. And now send men to Joppa, and call for one Simon, whose surname is Peter: He lodgeth with one Simon a tanner, whose house is by the sea side: he shall tell thee what thou oughtest to do.' And when the angel which spake unto Cornelius was departed, he called two of his household servants, and a devout soldier of them that waited on him continually; and when he had declared all these things unto them, he sent them to Joppa."

In these passages, we see Cornelius; a Gentile (someone outside the Jewish faith and not under the covenant of Yahuah) has just been converted into Yahuah's covenant when an angel appears to him instructing him to send for Peter to come to his house. Ordinarily, Peter would not have gone because Jews did not associate with Gentiles but because Yahuah had shown Peter that vision, he had no qualms in going. He now understands that he is to go and preach to Cornelius and his household, and that they will be baptized and receive the Holy Spirit. Yahuah shows Peter He had offered salvation to include the Gentiles and that was when Peter understands the vision. He even says this when he is talking with Cornelius by saying in Acts 10: 28, 34, *"And he said unto them, 'Ye know how that it is an unlawful thing for a man that is a Jew to keep company, or come unto one of another nation; but Yahuah hath showed me that I should not call any man common or unclean.'…Then Peter opened his mouth, and said, 'of a truth I perceive that Yahuah is no respecter of persons: But in every nation he that feareth him, and worketh righteousness, is accepted with him.'"*

Peter was one of Yeshua' disciples, and if Yeshua had cleansed all food, when Peter heard in the vision the voice asking him to eat, Peter would not have replied, "Not so, Yahuah; for I have never eaten anything that is common or unclean." He would have gone ahead and killed and eaten, since Yeshua cleansed all foods.

These passages quoted above in no way reflect a change in the laws of unclean foods. Yahuah simply used the vision of unclean animals to make a point to Peter: when He has spiritually cleansed someone typically considered unclean, the person should no longer be referred/seen as common or unclean."

Some people also cite 1 Timothy 4:1-5, saying Paul taught people that all meat is good for food. Let's look at that Scripture: *"Now the Spirit speaketh expressly, that in the latter times some shall depart from the faith, giving heed to seducing spirits, and doctrines of devils; speaking lies in hypocrisy; having their conscience seared with a hot iron; forbidding to marry, and commanding to abstain from meats, **which Yahuah hath created to be received with thanksgiving of them which believe and know the truth.** For every creature of Yahuah is good, and nothing to be refused, if it be received with thanksgiving: For it is sanctified by the word of Yahuah and prayer"* (emphasis mine).

In context, Paul warns Timothy of an apostasy that will occur in the end times, which would command abstinence from meats (foods) that Yahuah has declared as clean food (these unclean foods were never created to be eaten so this scripture does not apply to them, it applies to clean foods Yahuah created that we've been told are not good for us). We can see this happening like the Bible called it in today's world with the emergence of practices like plant-based eating, clean eating, and vegan diets. While I agree that our diet should consist more of fruits and vegetables, these are good in conjunction with eating toxic free and non processed meats. Yahuah, the Creator, gave us meat as food as seen in Genesis 9:3-4 (*....I have given them to you for food, just as I have given you grain and vegetables. But you must never eat any meat that still has the lifeblood in it* (NLT). Yahuah knows what's best for us, but man has brainwashed us to believe foods that are good for us i.e. meat including fish and chicken is bad and things we are not even supposed to eat are good for us. We have defiled Yahuah by incorporating unclean things into our diets. Shellfish and all other unclean animals have found their way onto our table when in actuality shellfish are bottom feeders — they feed on parasites and skin that they pick off dead things and when we eat them, we are essentially eating "dead things" thereby exposing our body to toxins we ordinarily wouldn't have if we hadn't been eating from the part of the earth we shouldn't be eating from.

These animals' purposes are to clean the seas and not to be used for food. Yes, they taste hella good, but this shows us that everything Yahuah makes is sublime, even the toilet of the seas.

Some say these laws of clean and unclean animals are part of the commandments given to Moses and no longer apply which is untrue. The laws of clean and unclean animals were set by Yahuah from the beginning of time, as seen in Genesis 7: 2-3: *"Of every clean beast thou shalt take to thee by sevens, the male and his female: and of beasts that are not clean by two, the male and his female. Of fowls also of the air by sevens, the male and the female; to keep seed alive upon the face of all the earth."* When the Israelites lived in Egypt, they kept to their dietary laws and when they got into the wilderness, Yahuah had Moses reiterate the laws to the Israelites because they were going into the Promised Land, the land of the Gentiles who didn't keep the dietary laws and He didn't want them eating unclean foods.

While the Bible never tells us why Yahuah gave us this law, most people have come to the conclusion that these laws were set to keep our bodies healthy and free from diseases and toxins due to microorganisms and parasites these unclean animals have in them. This makes one wonder if that's one of the reasons we have all types of non-sexual diseases that have no cure. I don't really know why Yahuah made these laws and neither do I care; what I do know is that in order for these animals to become clean, some things would have had to happen. 1) Yahuah would have had to go back on His Word. Yahuah said those unclean animals are an abomination to us (Leviticus 11:10-14) – once an abomination; always an abomination. Yahuah does not use that word for a lot of things but the things He used them on can NEVER become dear to Him. 2) These animals would have had to be re-created to include fins and scales, to chew the cud and to have split hooves. 3) Their purpose would have also had to change — scavengers, prey animals, cleaners of the seas, etc. would have also had to change but didn't.

Some people like to say Yahuah is progressive, so some things He hates, He may now like. No. Never! And I can relate to that. For instance, I DETEST slugs; they disgust me and make my skin crawl. One day, I was sitting in the yard drinking out of a mug. I went inside for a while and when I came back there was a slug in the mug. Yuck!! I felt my skin start to crawl, I grabbed the mug and thought of getting the slug out to keep the mug but I couldn't imagine ever drinking out of that mug again. I started walking towards the house to throw it in the trash and I thought, *"I don't want that in my house."* I took a plastic bag and threw the mug with the slug in the trashcan outside. I didn't want to have anything to do with something that I detest so much. I heard the Holy Spirit ask, "Why didn't you take the slug out and keep the mug?" I said I couldn't imagine me doing that; the thought made my skin crawl even more. I heard, "But the slug is no more in it and I'm sure once you wash it, you will be fine." I responded, "The fact that I know a slug was in that mug, my lips will never touch that mug ever again. That's gross" then I heard, "It's the same thing with Yahuah. You can clean up a sin/food/practice all you want, but underneath it all, it is still a sin." No matter how we may want to clean these foods and some sins up, they will always be an abomination to Yahuah and us and will forever remain unfit for human consumption.

To quote Ann Wigmore, a holistic health practitioner, "The food you eat can be either the safest and most powerful form of medicine or the slowest form of poison." Pick your food wisely!

Chapter 20

Death

Even though I walk through the darkest valley, I will fear no evil, for you are with me, your rod and your staff, they comfort me ~ Psalm 23:4 (NIV)

Death and taxes are the two things in life people say are constant and even though we see and hear about people dying around us every day, most of us still treat death like a taboo. We don't want to talk about it and are still afraid to die. Why? We have not accepted it because most of us are in denial that it can happen to us in the next second. We all experience life because Yahuah had a use for us on earth and whether we fulfil that purpose or not, we eventually have to go back to meet our Maker, either via death (which most of us will experience) or by rapture, when Yeshua comes back to take His people to heaven.

Heaven is our final destination, and life on earth we can say is the "layover at the airport" but most of us treat life like the final destination and unpack our bags at the airport, as if we are here to stay. Then we get extremely sad when the connecting flight (death) arrives to take people around us to their final destination. Don't get me wrong; death is *never* easy and will *never* be, especially if we keep treating it like a taboo. I've never seen someone happy that a loved one died, but I've seen them be at peace because they were prepared for it (even when it happened suddenly), and they know they will see them again when they get to heaven. Imagine what this world would be like if we all lived our lives embracing death; knowing it could happen any second, we wouldn't have time to hate or have any problems with people because we would be too preoccupied with living our lives to the fullest each and every day.

I used to be terrified of death for two reasons: I didn't want to leave my loved ones, and I was scared of feeling any pain (in case I didn't die peacefully in my sleep). One night, I was praying and talking to the Holy Spirit about death and why Yahuah allowed some people go through excruciating circumstances while dying. I was really in a great deal of pain because someone I loved died in a plane crash, and I didn't understand why they had to go in such a ghastly way. I was reminded of Psalm 23:4, *"Yea, though I walk through the valley of the shadow of death, I will fear no evil: for thou art with me; thy rod and thy staff they comfort me."* I had read that Scripture many times and I still didn't feel any comfort about dying. The Holy Spirit said to me, "Like that Scripture says, I am always with you, even in those excruciating painful times." But it still didn't make me feel better and I went to bed.

The next morning, I was on Facebook and I saw a story about a terrible accident that happened when a drunk driver slammed into another vehicle killing five passengers. My heart was heavy and I spoke to the Holy Spirit saying, *why did those innocent people have to die and in such a terrible painful way? I just don't get it.* I heard the Holy Spirit say, "Keep reading." Towards the end of the article, a witness at the accident scene said when the accident happened, he and the other people who witnessed the accident expected to hear a lot of screams and anguish from the people involved in the accident but there was nothing…just silence. They died instantly and didn't feel any pain (This was confirmed by the Medical Examiner). The Holy Spirit said, "Whenever Yahuah's people (people who believe in Yeshua) are involved in situations like that, they don't feel a thing because we always "pull their spirit out." Of course, to us, people who witness the aftermath, all we can see is the pain and anguish, especially since the accident resulted in death. We assume they felt pain. I started researching stories of people who were in accidents but didn't die to see if they felt any pain and it was consistent with what the Holy Spirit said. Nobody felt a thing. I personally know someone who got hit by a car and before the impact; he passed out and woke up at the hospital in really bad condition, but didn't remember the accident. Another girl I know got into a really bad car accident where a truck ran a red light and crushed her car. She passed out right before the impact and woke up two hours later as the Jaws of Life was working to get her out. It got me thinking, what of those people who had a near-death experience or died but felt every second of the pain, does that mean they don't or didn't belong to Yahuah? I may never know the answer to that but what I do know is, it is time for all of us to get right with Yahuah. Yeshua already conquered death so we have nothing to fear and no pain to feel.

There are differing beliefs about life after death. While some people have "died" and come back and told stories about heaven and hell, some people don't believe it and count those stories as fables, just like they count the Bible as a bunch of fairy tales. While I still have my reservations about stories of those going to heaven and coming back to earth because based on what the scriptures say, every person that has died so far is "sleeping" and are not in heaven yet (story for another day). I believe in Yahuah, Yeshua and the Holy Spirit as well as the Bible and Heaven and Hell and many people ask me why? The best answer I can give is this: "Yahuah has shown Himself in my life, my family, and situations time and time again so I am convinced and fully persuaded that He is REAL and that is good enough for me. Besides, I would rather live my life in the things of the Spirit (Galatians 5:22-23) which the world considers boring and my soul spending eternity in heaven, than living my life in sin which is sweet to the flesh but with eternal consequences of pain and anguish in hell.

"One day you will die! One day you will become part of the ultimate statistic. And when you die, you will face the biggest test of all. Will you go to heaven? The day you die, your beliefs about life after death, heaven and hell, will finally be put to the test—and you cannot afford to be wrong! Especially if hell is real and you go there. You might think, 'I don't believe in that stuff.' The day you die, THAT BELIEF will be tested, and you cannot afford to be wrong. Some say, 'Well, if there's a judgment day, I'm prepared to take my chances.' Is to gamble with the eternal destiny of your soul worth it? Why make such a gamble when to lose would mean to suffer everlasting torment in hell fire, in outer darkness and separated from everything that could remotely be called love? If you go to hell, you will not be partying with your friends. You will have no friends—forever" (From www.lifeafterdeath.net.nz).

This is not about what religion we practice or whether we believe heaven and hell are real. It's more about where our soul ends up on Judgment Day. This is why Yeshua came to earth, to take our sins away and conquer death. The Bible says in John 3:16, *"For Yahuah so loved the world that he gave his one and only Son, that whoever believes in him shall not perish but have eternal life"* (NIV). Do not delay for tomorrow might be too late. If you are ready to invite Yeshua into your life, pray the redemption prayer on page 135.

Chapter 21

Day of Judgment

When the master of the house has locked the door, it will be too late. You will stand outside knocking and pleading "Yeshua open the door for us! But He will reply, I don't know you or where you come from" ~ Luke 13:25 (NLT)

I'm here to remind everyone (myself included) that whether we believe it or not, the Day of Judgment will happen and it won't matter whether we want to participate or not—like death, it is inevitable and we don't get to choose. We must all stand judgment in front of Christ. He's the ONLY ONE who has the FINAL say.

We will be judged not only for the things we did, but also for the things we didn't do. Yahuah will judge us on whether we lived out the purpose for which He put us on this earth, if we honoured our parents, how we treated people, if we forbade to marry and for the ones that did marry, how we treated our spouses and upheld the principles of marriage, how we raised our children, how we used our faith and of course, our sins. Just like I was called to write this book as a reminder that this life will pass away sooner than later, there are several other people who have gotten the call and I believe it's because we are in the last days. Yahuah is warning us and we need to take heed. So to that I say guys, now is the time to get on the right side and get our names in the Book of Life so we can be one of the ones who enter into the New Jerusalem and not burn in the lake of fire and brimstone.

What is the New Jerusalem? It is the city where Yahuah will dwell with us; His people, for eternity. There will be no more tears; no more death, no more sorrow, and no more pain, for all those things will have passed away. The Bible depicts the New Jerusalem laid out like a square (although it's more of "a metropolis). "A 'city' of this size in the middle of the United States would stretch from Canada to Mexico and from the Appalachian Mountains to the California border. The New Jerusalem is all the square footage anyone could ask for." (*What Are the New Jerusalem's Dimensions?* By Randy Alcorn. *February 22, 2010*).

Can you believe how huge this city is? It's unreal! The city's radiance is described like a most rare jewel, like jasper, clear as crystal. The walls are great and high; it has 12 gates which are guarded by 12 angels, with names written on them (the names of the 12 tribes of the children of Israel); the wall of the city has 12 foundations, and in them the names of the 12 apostles of the Lamb. And the foundations of the wall of the city are garnished with all manner of precious stones. The first foundation is jasper; the second, sapphire; the third, a chalcedony; the fourth, an emerald; the fifth, sardonyx (onyx); the sixth, sardius (carnelian); the seventh, chrysolite; the eighth, beryl; the ninth, a topaz; the tenth, chrysoprasus (Chrysoprase); the eleventh, a jacinth; and the twelve, an amethyst. And the 12 gates are made of pearls—each gate from a single pearl (mind blowing) and the street of the city is pure gold, as if it is transparent glass. The city has no need of the sun or moon, for Yahuah's glory illuminates it and the Lamb is its light. Its gates will NEVER be closed at the end of day because there shall be no night there (Revelation 21).

I'm pretty sure we would all love to be in the brilliance and splendour of this city (I know I do), and we can, as long as our names are in the Book of Life. If your name isn't in it as of this moment, no worries, it can be added. Start by introducing yourself to Yeshua, and say the redemption prayer on page 135. You can begin the process of walking with Yeshua now because tomorrow might be too late.

Please, understand that this is not an attempt to throw you or anyone into panic mode, but it is a call to action for us to accept Yeshua's sacrificial death for our sins, to ask Him to come into our lives, and then to begin to live right. Revelation

21:7-8 tells us, "*He who overcomes [the world by adhering faithfully to Christ Yeshua as Lord and Saviour] will inherit these things; and I will be his father, and he will be my son. But as for the cowards and unbelieving and abominable [who are devoid of character and personal integrity and practice or tolerate immorality], and murderers, and whoremongers, and sorcerers [with intoxicating drugs], and idolaters and occultists [who practice and teach false religions], and all the liars [who knowingly deceive and twist truth], their part will be in the lake that blazes with fire and brimstone, which is the second death*" [AMP].

I feel the need to also say this; please take into account that there is a difference in you knowing someone of importance and someone of importance knowing you. For example, most of us believe we "know" people just by watching them on TV, but unless we have a personal relationship with them, we don't truly know them and they are nothing more than "friends in our heads." Say, for example, you feel you 'know' President Buhari (Nigeria) and think you are kindred spirits because of all you've seen and read about him so you set out to see him. You get in front of his house and ask to speak with him; ten times out of ten, you will be denied access because he doesn't know you but if he does know you, you will gain access to him immediately.

It's the same concept with Yahuah. Many of us believe we have a personal relationship and access to Yahuah, Yeshua and the Holy Spirit because we can quote Scripture, we read the Bible, we attend church regularly, we pray, we heal people, we

help people, etc. but just because we do those things does not mean they know us. Matthew 7:21-23 says, "*Not everyone who calls out to me, Yeshua, Yeshua will enter*
the Kingdom of Heaven. Only those who actually do the will of my father in heaven will enter. On judgment day, many will say to me 'Yeshua, Yeshua! We prophesied in your name and cast out demons in your name and performed many miracles in your name.' But I will reply, 'I never knew you, get away from me, you who breaks Yahuah's laws'" (NLT). The Bible, in Revelation 21:27, tells us, "*Nothing unclean and no one who does shameful things or tell lies will ever go into the New Jerusalem. Only those whose names are written in the Lamb's book of life will enter the city*" (NCV). It is important that they (Yahuah, Yeshua and the Holy Spirit) know you and the only way they will is by repenting of your sins, thanking Yeshua for His sacrificial death, accepting Him as your Saviour, fellowshipping with them daily and then letting the Holy Spirit lead and guide you in His ways.

HE, WHO HAS EARS, LET HIM HEAR!

***

The seven messages to the churches in the book of Revelations are supposed to convey the information that the body of Christ need to hear as well as prepare the body of Christ for the end time. I believe it is imperative to read through each one as it shows us how we are failing in our calling to be Ambassadors of Christ. Christ has given us promises and warnings but these are being neglected so I suggest you read through and let the Holy Spirit minister to you.

The Loveless Church (Revelation 2:1-7)

To the angel of the church of Ephesus write, 'These things says He who holds the seven stars in His right hand, who walks in the midst of the seven golden lampstand: "I know your works, your labour, your patience, and that you cannot bear those who are evil. And you have tested those who say they are apostles and are not, and have found them liars; and you have persevered and have patience, and have laboured for my name's sake and have not become weary. Nevertheless I have this against you, that you have left your first love. Remember therefore from where you have fallen; repent and do the first works, or else I will come to you quickly and remove your lampstand from its place – unless you repent. But this you have, that you hate the deeds of the Nicolaitans, which I also hate. "He, who has an ear, let him hear what the Spirit says to the churches. To him who overcomes I will give to eat from the tree of life, which is in the midst of Yahuah's Paradise" (NKJV).

The Persecuted Church (Revelation 2: 8-11)

And to the angel of the church in Smyrna write, 'these things says the First and the Last, who was dead, and came to life: "I know your works, tribulation, and poverty {but you are rich}; and I know the blasphemy of those who say they are Jews and are not, but are a synagogue of Satan. Do not fear any of those things which you are about to suffer. Indeed, the devil is about to throw some of you into prison, that you may be tested, and you will have tribulation ten days. Be faithful until death, and I will give you the crown of life. "He, who has an ear, let him hear what the Spirit says to the churches. He who overcomes shall not be hurt by the second death" (NKJV).

The Compromising Church (Revelation 2: 12-17)
And to the angel of the church in Pergamos write, 'these things says He who has the sharp two-edged sword: "I know your works, and where you dwell, where Satan's throne is. And you hold fast to My name, and did not deny My faith even in the days in which Antipas was My faithful martyr, who was killed among you, where Satan dwells. But I have a few things against you, because you have there those who hold the doctrine of Balaam, who taught Balak to put a stumbling block before the children of Israel, to eat things sacrificed to idols, and to commit sexual immorality. Thus you also have those who hold the doctrine of the Nicolaitans, which thing I hate. Repent, or else I will come to you quickly and will fight against them with the sword of My mouth. "He who has an ear, let him hear what the Spirit says to the churches. To him who overcomes I will give some of the hidden manna to eat. And I will give him a white stone, and on the stone a new name written which no one knows except him who receives it (NKJV).

The Corrupt Church (Revelation 2: 18-29)
And to the angel of the church in Thyatira write, 'These things says the Son of Yahuah, who has eyes like a flame of fire, and His feet like fine brass: "I know your works, love, service, faith, and your patience;

and as for your works, the last are more than the first. Nevertheless I have a few things against you, because you allow that woman Jezebel, who calls herself a prophetess, to teach and seduce My servants to commit sexual immorality and eat things sacrificed to idols. And I gave her time to repent of her sexual immorality, and she did not repent. Indeed I will cast her into a sickbed, and those who commit adultery with her into great tribulation, unless they repent of their deeds. I will kill her children with death, and all the churches shall know that I am He who searches the minds and hearts. And I will give to each one of you according to your works. "Now to you I say, and to the rest in Thyatira, as many as do not have this doctrine, who have not known the depths of Satan, as they say, I will put on you no other burden. But hold fast what you have till I come. And he who overcomes, and keeps My works until the end, to him I will give power over the nations — 'He shall rule them with a rod of iron; They shall be dashed to pieces like the potter's vessels' — as I also have received from My Father; and I will give him the morning star. "He who has an ear, let him hear what the Spirit says to the churches (NKJV).

The Dead Church (Revelation 3: 1-6)

And to the angel of the church in Sardis write, 'these things say He who has the seven Spirits of Yahuah and the seven stars: "I know your works, that you have a name that you are alive, but you are dead. Be watchful, and strengthen the things which remain, that are ready to die, for I have not found your works perfect before Yahuah. Remember therefore how you have received and heard; hold fast and repent. Therefore if you will not watch, I will come upon you as a thief, and you will not know what hour I will come upon you. You have a few names even in Sardis who have not defiled their garments; and they shall walk with Me in white, for they are worthy. He who overcomes shall be clothed in white garments, and I will not blot out his name from the Book of Life; but I will confess his name before My Father and before His angels. "He who has an ear, let him hear what the Spirit says to the churches" (NKJV).

The Faithful Church (Revelation 3: 7-13)

And to the angel of the church in Philadelphia write, 'These things says He who is holy, He who is true, "He who has the key of David, He who opens and no one shuts, and shuts and no one opens": "I know your works. See, I have set before you an open door, and no one can shut it; for you have a little strength, have kept My word, and have not denied My name. Indeed I will make those of the synagogue of Satan, who say they are Jews and are not, but lie — indeed I will make them come and worship before your feet, and to know that I have loved you. Because you have kept My command to persevere, I also will keep you from the hour of trial which shall come upon the whole world, to test those who dwell on the earth. Behold, I am coming quickly! Hold fast what you have, that no one may take your crown. He who overcomes, I will make him a pillar in the temple of My Yahuah, and he shall go out no more. I will write on him the name of Yahuah and the name of the city of My Yahuah, the New Jerusalem, which comes down out of heaven from My Yahuah. And I will write on him My new name. "He who has an ear, let him hear what the Spirit says to the churches" (NKJV).

The Lukewarm Church (Revelation 3:14-22)

And to the angel of the church of the Laodiceans write, 'these things says the Amen, the Faithful and True Witness, the Beginning of the creation of Yahuah: "I know your works, that you are neither cold nor hot. I could wish you were cold or hot. So then, because you are lukewarm, and neither cold nor hot, I will vomit you out of My mouth. Because you say, 'I am rich, have become wealthy, and have need of nothing' — and do not know that you are wretched, miserable, poor, blind, and naked — I counsel you to buy from Me gold refined in the fire, that you may be rich; and white garments, that you may be clothed, that the shame of your nakedness may not be revealed; and anoint your eyes with eye salve, that you may see. As many as I love, I rebuke and chasten. Therefore be zealous and repent. Behold, I stand at the door and knock. If anyone hears My voice and opens the door, I will come in to him and dine with him, and he with Me. To him who overcomes I will grant to sit with Me on My throne, as I also overcame and sat down with My Father on His throne. "He who has an ear, let him hear what the Spirit says to the churches (NKJV).

Chapter 22

Arsenals

Be sober, be vigilant; because your adversary the devil, as a roaring lion walketh about, seeking whom he may devour ~ 1 Peter 5:8

Yahuah has equipped us for life by giving us principles and things that, if used, will make our lives better on earth. I refer to these principles and things as arsenals and they include: Yeshua; the Holy Spirit; the Bible; Speaking, Faith; Heavenly Language; Prayer/Meditation; and Angels.

The Holy Spirit: The Holy Spirit is the Comforter; Advocate, and Counsellor whom Yeshua promised to give us. The Bible says in Luke 11:9-13, *"And I say unto you, Ask, and it shall be given you; seek, and ye shall find; knock, and it shall be opened unto you. For every one that asketh receieveth; and he that seeketh findeth; and to him that knocketh it shall be opened. If a son shall ask bread of any of you that is a father, will he give him a stone? Or if he ask a fish, will he for fish give him a serpent? Or if he shall ask an egg, will he offer him a scorpion? If ye then, being evil, know how to give good gifts unto your children: how much more shall your heavenly Father give the Holy Spirit to them that ask him?"*

Once the Holy Spirit comes to reside in us, He never leaves us. He guides and leads us into Yahuah's truth. Now even though the Holy Spirit comes to live in us, He will not invade our lives. We have to ask Him to help us, by speaking it out loud. This is not a one-time thing, it's not even a daily thing; it's a continuous process, a moment-by-moment process. While the Holy Spirit lives in us, He will not go to work till we do two things: give Him permission to take control and speak the things we want Him to change in our lives.

The Bible (Yahuah's Word)

In order to grow in our relationship with Christ, it is imperative we read His word so we know how to interact with Him as well as know His promises for us. Reading the Bible also shows us Yahuah's character and answers a lot of questions we may have about Him and this world we live in. It's even more important to read His word now more than ever because we have a lot of false teachings out there and as Yahuah's word never changes, we can be sure to discern the truth from reading the Word. Many verses in Scripture point to how important it is to know Yahuah's Word. One of them is found in Joshua 1:8 *"Keep this book of the law always on your lips, meditate on it day and night, so that you may be careful to do everything written in it. Then you will be prosperous and successful"* (NIV). FYI: Meditation in this context is not referring to Transcendental Meditation which is a technique for detaching oneself from anxiety and promoting harmony and self-realization by repetition of a mantra, and other yogic practices; rather it is referring to reading the Scriptures and focusing on the Holy Spirit to help shed light on what has been read so as to understand it deeply. In the past, I could not understand why I needed to memorize Scripture, but then the Holy Spirit showed me several reasons why. 1) We can triumph over Satan when he comes to mess with us just like Yeshua did (Luke 4: 1-13). 2) Our prayers are more powerful when we pray using scriptures. 3) We can flee from sin/temptation when we combat it with scriptures. 4) We can test the spirit. 5) We can petition Yahuah with his own words and "remind" Him of those promises He made just like King David did in Psalm 119:49-50, *"Remember the word unto thy servant, upon which thou has caused me to hope. This is my comfort in my affliction: for thy word hath quickened me."* There are several other reasons for memorising Scripture which I hope you will find out as you study and memorise His word.

Prayer and meditation go hand in hand. Prayer according to the world is a "solemn request for help or an expression of thanks addressed to Yahuah or an object of worship" (Google). Solemn prayer is a type of prayer, but it's not all of what prayer is about. Prayer as Yahuah intended is a way of communication between Him and us; i.e. talking to Him and having a conversation. If our prayer lives involve us only saying solemn request prayers, then we are in trouble. Some of us have been conditioned to see prayer as that long, boring activity people do, which we hate every minute of; but if we really understand the gravity of what is happening whenever praying is happening around us, we would take advantage of those moments. The Bible tells us in Ephesians 6:12, *"For we wrestle not against flesh and blood, but against principalities, against powers, against the rulers of the darkness of this world, against spiritual wickedness in high places."* So we have to *"be unceasing and persistent in prayer"* (1 Thessalonians 5:17 AMP)

Prayer is a cloth of protection we wear and something we need like air and until we recognize that, we will always leave each day's blessings, protection, favour, provision and wisdom etc. on the table of life and be left wondering why we have so many challenges in life.

Speaking
Most of us have issues, dreams, goals, etc. we think of in our minds. We might even write some of these things down but

never speak them out loud. Genesis 1:2 says, *"The earth was without form, and void; and darkness was on the face of the deep. And the Spirit of Yahuah was hovering over the face of the waters"* (NKJV).

Genesis Chapter 1:3-31 shows us that when Yahuah spoke, commanding something to be, it was so. Why is that? The Holy Spirit went to work. Genesis 1:2 tells us that the Holy Spirit was "hovering" (waiting near at hand). Picture a plane or helicopter hovering. It's ready to land but still has to wait on commands to do that. This is similar to what was happening when Yahuah was creating the earth; The Holy Spirit was ready to go to work but had to wait on Yahuah to speak. As soon as Yahuah spoke, He went into action! And everything Yahuah said to be *"was as requested and good!"* (Genesis 1: 1-25).

Proverbs 18:20- 21, 7 says, *"A man's belly shall be satisfied with the fruit of the tongue: and with the increase of his lips shall he be filled. Death and life are in the power of the tongue: and they that love it shall eat the fruit thereof."* In order words, *"People will be rewarded for what they say; they will be rewarded by how they speak. What you say can mean life or death. Those who speak with care will be rewarded. The words of fools will ruin them; their own words will trap them"* (NCV) and we see this in the life of certain people in the Bible; the woman with the issue of blood spoke life, the centurion servant spoke life, Daniel spoke life, the three Jewish boys (Shadrach, Meshach, and Abednego) spoke life; need I go on?

So what are we speaking? Are we speaking life or death into our situations? Are we speaking what our eyes can see or what we are hoping for? Nine times out of ten, we are speaking fear so we end up getting more of what we don't want instead of what we want. The book of Job shows something interesting about Job's situation. We always celebrate Job's restoration but we ignore something Job said. In Job 3:25(NLT), he said, *"Everything I feared and dreaded has happened to me."* Job lived in fear hence why he kept making sacrifices. Job 1:5 (NIV) tells us, *"...Early in the morning he would sacrifice a burnt offering for each of them, thinking, **"Perhaps my children have sinned and cursed Yahuah in their hearts."'*** This was job's regular custom" (emphasis mine). Job was a good man, a religious man who did the right things but for the wrong reasons. He did what Yahuah asked for, not out of praise and thanksgiving to Yahuah. It was out of fear, out of what he thought his children were doing wrong. Alas, all the things Job thought and spoke happened to him even though all the while he "thought" he was doing the right thing by offering sacrifices. His children died and he lost EVERYTHING! But during his trial, Job learnt that Yahuah's ways are not our ways and everything he thought he knew about Yahuah and life were wrong. Yahuah restored him and *blessed the last part of Job's life even more than the first part* because I presume Job started speaking life and having the right thoughts and so he lived happily ever after.

We have to ask ourselves, are we like Job? Are we thinking the wrong thoughts, speaking the wrong things and obeying Yahuah's commands (going to church, giving, going to Bible study, reading the Bible, and tithing) out of fear of what could happen? Why live in that world when you can live in faith and honour Yahuah. Fear and Faith cannot live in the same world. It's impossible. They are both laws and operate in the same way. They are both asking us to believe in what hasn't happened yet and both have a 50/50 chance of happening as whatever fear or faith words we think or speak is what will gravitate towards us. Let's make it a habit of speaking life, thinking positive thoughts and communicating with the Holy Spirit, so He can go to work on cleaning up our lives for the better.

Faith

Faith as defined on Google is "a strong belief in Yahuah." Although we say we have a strong belief in Yahuah, when we pay attention to the way we live, most of us live like we have a stronger belief in fear. The thing most people don't understand about Yahuah's Kingdom is this: there is no anxiety or fear— these things don't exist there. If you are a believer and are plagued with worry, doubt, anxiety, fear, etc. know that these things are from the enemy and cannot coexist with Yahuah's beliefs. Yahuah gives a peace and a knowing that no matter what happens, things will always work out for our good because of the Law of faith. The Bible tells us in Romans 3:27, *"Where is boasting then? It is excluded. By what law? Of works? No, but by the **law of faith"*** (emphasis mine). What is the law of faith? The law of faith as told in Hebrews 11:1 (NCV) *"means being sure of the things we hope for and knowing that something is real even if we do not see it;"* in other words, if you *believe* in and **expect** what you say, it will happen. This is not a maybe; it is a given. "Just like we have the laws of gravity, aerodynamics, electricity, sounds, etc., if we operate within any of the principles of these laws, it is safe, it performs well, and it is dependable. However, if we break those laws, we might be killed" (Culled from *Faith is a Law* by Tim Greenwood).

Likewise, with the Law of Faith, if you operate within its principles, it too, will be safe, perform for you, and will be something to depend on. For example, if you throw a ball out of a building, you know the law of gravity will come into play, causing the ball to drop. It's not whether it will happen; it's how soon it will happen. It is a given. The same thing goes for faith; if you follow the "rules" of faith, you will have your desired outcome.

Mark 11:22-23 says, *"And Yeshua answering saith unto them, 'Have faith in Yahuah. For verily I say unto you, that whosoever shall say unto this mountain, 'Be thou removed, and be thou cast into the sea; and shall not doubt in his heart, but shall believe that those things which he saith shall come to pass; he shall have whatsoever he saith.'"* Your "mountain" may be a problem, a challenge, a crisis, etc. Look what Yeshua says about the mountain! *YOU* can move it! You only have to command it to! Mark 11: 24 continues, *"Therefore, I say unto you, what things soever ye desire, when ye pray, believe that ye receive them and ye shall have them.'"* And we understand from studying Scripture that asking needs to be in line with Yahuah's Word.

- **Facts about Faith**

  Yahuah uses faith as a humility tool: Romans 12:3 says, *"...to every man that is among you, **not to think of himself more highly than he ought to think**; but to think soberly, according as Yahuah hath dealt to every man the measure of faith"* (emphasis mine). Nobody has more faith than the other. The only difference is the *strength* of our faith. It's the same way you can have two people at the same weight but with different strengths because one exercises and the other person doesn't. We can strengthen our faith but cannot increase it. We see this principle at play in Luke 17:6, *"If ye had faith as a grain of mustard seed, ye might say unto this sycamine tree, Be thou plucked up by the root, and be thou planted in the sea; and it should obey you.'"* It's not how much faith we have; it's how strong our faith is.

- ***Faith is a measure of criteria Yahuah will use to judge us***

  Yahuah will ask, why didn't you use your faith or why did you choose to use it in a limited way when people with the same amount of faith did magnificent things to further my Kingdom? If they could do that with the same amount of faith you have, what is your excuse?

What do we need for faith to work?

We need love, belief, the goal, corresponding action, expectation and imagination. The Bible tells us in Galatians 5:6,

"When we are in Christ…The important thing is faith – the kind of faith that works through love" (NCV). Faith is not working for some people because they do not love people outside of their close-knit circle. They love those they know and treat people they don't know like dirt, yet expect their faith to work. Another important thing needed for faith to work is WORKS. James 2:14-18 says, *"What does it profit, my brethren, **if someone says he has faith but does not have works**? Can faith save him? If a brother or sister is naked and destitute of daily food, and one of you says to them, 'Depart in peace, be warmed and filled,' but you do not give them the things which are needed for the body, what does it profit? Thus also **faith by itself, if it does not have works, is dead**. But someone will say, 'You have faith, and I have works. **Show me your faith without your works, and I will show you my faith by my works'"*** (NKJV; emphasis mine).

What are the actions behind your dreams or goals? Some people, for instance, say they believe for the fruit of the womb, but in my opinion, they do not really believe; they are merely praying. Believing for a baby will mean you have your body ready to receive a baby, you have a name picked out, you've bought some clothes, you've picked out the baby room theme—heck, the baby's room is done! Now, that is faith in action, walking by faith and not by sight. We have to start putting actions behind our faith. Yes, it might seem crazy to other people but the Bible tells us, in 2 Corinthians 5:7, *"For we walk by faith, not by sight."* Most of us would rather walk by sight rather than faith, especially when we are believing for healing, but in the words of Pastor Kenneth Copeland, "To consult your physical senses for evidence to answered prayer is as foolish as trying to smell with our ears."

Last but not least, we need to **expect** that our prayers have been answered. Most people say we should not expect anything as it is better to be surprised than to be disappointed but faith without expectation is not faith that is wishful thinking. Faith is being able to see what you have prayed about in your mind's eye i.e. imagining you have acquired it. I always say "why worry about things/situations you can't change when you can imagine the situation you want." It is a naïve way to look at things but if you are going to be a follower of Christ, you have to become like a child (Matthew 18:3). This is not suggesting we become immature but more so taking Yahuah's word as truth just like how children have a way of believing everything we tell them and accepting them as fact. Expect and act like your prayers have been answered and they will be.

Heavenly Language — Speaking in Tongues

There are a lot of controversies when it comes to speaking in tongues. Some people are for it and some against. I am totally for it because Yeshua tells us in Mark 16:17, "*And these signs shall follow them that believe; in my name shall they cast out devils;* **they shall speak with new tongues.**" (emphasis mine). 1 Corinthians 14:2 also tells us, "*for he that speaketh in an unknown tongue speaketh not unto men, but unto Yahuah: for no man understandeth him; howbeit in the spirit he speaketh mysteries.*" Do not sell yourself short. Follow after Yahuah, desire spiritual gifts, and He will give them to you.

Angels

All of us have angels keeping watch over us as told in several scriptures. Psalm 91:10 says, *"There shall no evil befall thee, neither shall any plague come nigh thy dwelling. For he shall give his angels charge over thee, to keep thee in all thy ways. They shall bear thee up in their hands, lest thou dash thy foot against a stone."* In order words, *"nothing bad will happen to you, no disaster will come to your home. He has put His angels in charge of you to watch over you wherever you go. They will catch you in their hands so that you will not hit your foot on a rock"* (NCV). Exodus 23:20 tells us *"See, I am sending an angel before you to protect you on your journey and lead you safely to the place I have prepared for you. Pay close attention to him, and obey his instructions. Do not rebel against him, for he is my representative, and he will not forgive your rebellion. But if you are careful to obey him, following all my*

instructions, then I will be an enemy to your enemies, and I will oppose those you oppose you" (NLT). Matthew 18:10 also tells us *"Take heed that ye despise not one of these little ones; for I say unto you, That in heaven their angels do always behold the face of my Father which is in heaven."*

FYI: This is in no way encouraging angel worship but to bring awareness to the fact that Yahuah has angels watching over us. The Bible tells us in Colossians 2:18 *"Let no one defraud you of your prize [your freedom in Christ and your salvation] by insisting on* *mock humility **and the worship of angels**....*" [AMP] (emphasis mine). Even an angel confirmed they (angels) should not be worshipped in Revelation 22:8-9 "*...I fell down to worship before the feet of the angel who showed me these things. But he said to me, 'Do not do that. I am a fellow servant with you and your brother's the prophet and with those who heed and remember [the truths contained in] the words of this book. Worship Yahuah'*" (AMP).

Angels are Yahuah's servants and are there to do His bidding i.e. protecting and serving followers of Christ as told in Hebrew 1:14 "Are not the angels ministering spirits sent out [by Yahuah] to serve (accompany, protect) those who will inherit salvation? [Of course they are!]"

***

Please people, let's get to accepting and believing the arsenals Yahuah gave us and use them to our advantage.

Chapter 23

Final Word

Life is a red twizzler — that twists and turns, with ups and downs; sometimes sweet and other times sour-But it always comes round full circle ~ unknown

Sometimes I try to rationalise everything the Holy Spirit revealed to me in this book with my carnal mind, I want to count it all as figments of my imagination — something my mind made up as I've sometimes been told. But that does not sit right with my spirit. Know why? Because when I re-read all that I wrote, I am still in awe because some of the Scriptures and topics I wrote about in this book, I had no previous knowledge of. The Holy Spirit somehow revealed them to me in order for me to write them down. What I know more than anything is this: I believe everything written here because I'm convinced they are the things Yahuah wants us to know so we can be prepared for what is coming.

Everything has come full circle for me. Those moments I had as a child with Yahuah where He would tell me I was destined for greatness, have arrived. This book is how He intends to use me. Yahuah is about to move and He chose me to deliver the message. Yes, little ol' me! Yahuah chose the same Bola Coker that has been through some trials (even if some were self-inflicted by making the wrong decisions regardless of how valid my reasons were for choosing to do them). I've learnt that "Freedom of choice does not mean freedom from consequences," I've been there, done that; and if I could do things differently, I would. However, I don't regret anything I've done because at some point, it was exactly what I wanted or needed. Everything that has happened to me has made me into the woman I am today.

Yahuah on the other hand continues to show Himself as a no respecter of persons as I've asked several times why He chose me of all people—with my past and present sins, my flaws and what people thought about me. And I don't know if I will ever get an answer other than, He just did. I remember saying to the Holy Spirit, "No one will believe Yahuah sent me, of all people," and I heard, "Do not worry about people believing you." And then He brought a verse to my remembrance, "*A prophet is honoured everywhere except in his own hometown and with his own people and in his own home"* (Mark 6:4 NCV). People didn't believe Yeshua with all His signs and wonders. Don't expect them to believe you. Your job is to deliver a message and then it's up to them to decide if they will focus on the message and make some positive changes, or if they will focus on judging the messenger.

Message to the Doubters and Naysayers
My hope is you, the reader, will be open-minded and let the Holy Spirit convict you. You see, once you get finished reading this book and set it down, my mission is accomplished. I get a check mark for a job well done for accepting the call and delivering the message. But I do have to ask: PLEASE, PLEASE, PLEASE, **Don't Miss Out on Knowing Yahuah** even in your doubt, unbelief, judgments and possibly hate. Will you consider getting to know Yahuah? Maybe try it as an experiment to see if you can prove Yahuah doesn't exist (if that makes you feel better); whatever the case; do it. A terrible time is coming and the Bible story of Moses and the Egyptians is about to play out right in front of our eyes. Only you can decide which team you are going to be on. Are you going to be on the Israelites' or the Egyptians' team? On another note, some people may not even get to be on teams because death may come calling. Do you know where you will end up on Judgment Day? Are you ready to defend your life in order to make it through the pearly gates and into the New Jerusalem? Think about it, and please be prepared.

Accept Yeshua as your Saviour, believe in Him and start showing love to everyone you meet. Be a ray of sunshine to them as the Bible tells us in 2 Corinthians 4:6, *"For Yahuah, who commanded the light to shine out of darkness, hath shined in our hearts, to give the light of the knowledge of the glory of Yahuah in the face of Yeshua Christ."* We should be bursting with the light of love of Christ and be sharing that with people. Can you imagine if every person on this earth pledged to be a peacemaker and a ray of light to everyone they met, regardless of their differences? This world would so rock!

I pray that all of us will start to live out our purpose and advance Yahuah's Kingdom. Like Les Brown says, *"The wealthiest place on earth is the graveyard because there lays all the hopes and dreams of people that were never realised."* I pray that will not be your case, and you will decide to share yourself with the world by showcasing your gifts. If there is anything life has taught me, it is this: *You cannot isolate any situation that has happened to you, whether good or bad,* because Romans 8:28 tells us *"And we know that ALL THINGS WORK TOGETHER FOR GOOD TO THEM THAT LOVE YAHUAH, to them who are the called according to his purpose.* It is also important to know that, *"It's not where you start from that matters but where you finish"* (Zig Ziglar).

Finally, I leave you with the words of King Solomon (the wisest man who ever lived), he says in Ecclesiastes 8:16, *"I tried to understand all that happens on earth. I saw how busy people are, working day and night and hardly ever sleeping. I also saw all that Yahuah has done. Nobody can understand what Yahuah does here on earth. No matter how hard people try to understand it, they cannot. Even if wise people say they understand, they cannot: no one can really understand it"* (NCV). He gives his own advice to mankind at the end of the book in Ecclesiastes 12:13-14 saying *"Fear Yahuah and keep His commandments: for this is the whole duty of man. For Yahuah shall bring every work into judgment, with every secret thing, whether it be good, or whether it be evil."*

THEY WERE WARNED, JUST LIKE WE ARE.

³ For there is going to come a time when people won't listen to the truth, but will go around looking for teachers who will tell them just what they want to hear. ⁴ They won't listen to what the Bible says but will blithely follow their own misguided ideas

2 Timothy 4:3-4 (TLB)

HE WHO HAS EARS, LET THEM HEAR!

MESSAGE TO NIGERIA

Chapter 24

Message to Nigeria

"The Sins of the people of Israel and Judah are very, very great.
The entire land is full of murder, the city filled with injustice.
They are saying, "The Lord doesn't see it! The Lord has
abandoned the land!' So I will not spare them or have any pity
on them. I will fully repay them for all they have done."
~ Ezekiel 9:9-10

When I was done writing this book, I was outside in my backyard praying, asking Yahuah about the next steps for this book, when I heard, "Release the book in Nigeria before you make it available anywhere else."My response, "Say, what now? Nigeria?! Why would I want to do that? I live in America, not Nigeria."

The Holy Spirit's response was, "Yahuah says, '*Like the groaning of the children of Israel when they were in bondage and I remembered my covenant with Abraham, with Isaac, and with Jacob; and looked upon the children of Israel, and acknowledged them* (See Exodus 2:23-25), *so have I heard the cry of the few 'righteous' Nigerians who weep and sigh in their difficulties because of the detestable sins being committed in their city and I have acknowledged it. It is time to act on their behalf so I am ushering Nigeria to become the Giant of Africa she was destined to be but before then, they will be a cleansing (judgment on the unrighteous) so I am sending you to your people, so go and release the book there first.*"

Later on that day, I discussed this some more with the Holy Spirit. I said, "I don't mean to be disrespectful or anything but *"you people" are adding to this assignment*? This was not part of the job description when I accepted to write this book; so now I have to give *a message of judgment and restoration directed to a whole country?*"

I heard, "You have no idea what you've signed up for?"

"What have I gotten myself into?" I thought. Then I heard the Holy Spirit say, "Be of good cheer; you are not the first person who have and will share this message."

I responded with "What do you mean?"

I heard, "I'm giving you an assignment: I want you to read the Book of Ezekiel and then look up all the prophecies you can find concerning Nigeria and you'll see what I mean."

I did just that, and can I say I was stunned?! The Book of Ezekiel read like I was looking into a mirror and seeing what is happening in present-day Nigeria. I also found numerous prophecies concerning Nigeria on the Internet. I took that back to the Holy Spirit and said, "The Book of Ezekiel promises judgment and restoration for Jerusalem and other nations and the prophecies I found are all about restoration so what is the message you want me to share?

The Holy Spirit said, "Exactly what the Book of Ezekiel is about, judgment for Nigeria (which has already started if you open your eyes to see what's currently happening) and the restoration that will soon follow."

This left me speechless because Nigeria is a nation of people who love Yahuah; there are churches on every corner you turn; I can comfortably say that we are the most prayerful nation in the world so why would Yahuah want to pass judgment on us as a nation? The scripture tells us in James 5:16 that the *"prayers of a righteous man availeth much,"* meaning the prayers of a righteous (holy) person has great power and produces wonderful results. Yet we don't see that happening in Nigeria, we pray and nothing happens. Wonder why? Our prayers aren't earnest (showing sincere and intense conviction) and we are immoral and disobedient. We claim we love Yahuah and are followers of Christ but we have become immoral. Yes, we've become sexually impure, thieves, pimps, murderers, swindlers, yahoo boys, Boko Haram, 419ers; we are shepherded by false prophets and corrupt leaders; we love bribes and will do these vicious things openly because we have no shame. To say it as best as I can, **Nigeria has gone to the gutters** and are like the people talked about in James 4:2-10, *"We want what we don't have so we scheme and kill to get it. We are jealous of what others have, but we can't get it, so we fight and wage war to take it away from them. Yet we don't have what we want because we don't ask Yahuah for it. And even when we ask, we don't get it because our motives are all wrong — we want only what will give us pleasure. You adulterers! (Yahuah says) Don't you realise that friendship with the world makes you my enemy? I say again: if you want to be a friend of the world, you make yourself my enemy. Do you think the scriptures have no meaning? They say that Yahuah is passionate that the spirit he has placed within us should be faithful to him. And he gives grace generously. As the Scriptures say, 'Yahuah opposes the proud but gives grace to the humble.' So humble yourselves before Yahuah. Resist the devil, and he will flee from you. Come close to Yahuah, and He will come to you. Wash your hands, you sinners; purify your heart, for your loyalty is divided between Yahuah and the world. Let there be tears for what you have done. Let there be sorrow and deep grief. Let there be sadness instead of laughter, and gloom instead of joy. Humble yourselves before Yahuah and he will lift you up in honour."*

It is time for us to turn from our evil and immoral ways and become "true" followers of Yeshua and live by His commands. Deuteronomy 28:1-14 (NCV) tells us exactly how Yahuah will restore Nigeria if we fully obey and carefully keep all His commands. *"And Yahuah will make you greater than any nation on earth. Obey Yahuah so that these blessings will come and stay with you. You will be blessed in the city and blessed in the country. Your children will be blessed, as well as your crops; your herds will be blessed with calves and your flocks with lambs. Your basket and your kitchen will be blessed. You will be blessed when you come and when you go out. Yahuah will help you defeat the enemies that come to fight you. They will attack you from one direction, but they will run from you in seven directions. Yahuah will bless you with full barns, and he will bless everything you do. He will bless the land he is giving you. Yahuah will make you his holy people, as he promised. But you must obey his commands and do what he wants you to do. Then everyone on earth will see that you are Yahuah's people, and they will be afraid of you. The lord will make you rich: You will have many children, your animals will have many young, and your land will give good crops. It is the land Yahuah promised your ancestors he will give to you. Yahuah will open up his heavenly storehouse so that the skies send rain on your land at the right time, and he will bless everything you do. You will lend to other nations, but you will not need to borrow from them. He will make you the head and not the tail; you will be on top and not the bottom. But you must obey Yahuah's commands that I am giving you today, being careful to keep them. Do not obey anything I command you today. Do exactly as*

I command, and do not follow other gods or serve them." The Book of Ezekiel and Deut. 28:15-68 tells us exactly how He will judge the nation so please read at your leisure (highly important).

Yahuah says, *"If the wicked people turn away from all their sins and begin to obey my decrees and do what is just and right, they will surely live and not die. All their past sins will be forgotten, and they will live because of the righteous things they have done. Do you think that I like to see wicked people die? Says Yahuah. Of course not! I want them to turn from their wicked ways and live"* (Ezekiel 18:22-23, NLT). *"...He that heareth, let him hear; and he that forebeareth, let him forebear: for they are a rebellious house"* (Ezekiel 3:27).

Prophecies on Nigeria and Africa

Here are some of the previous prophecies concerning Nigeria pulled from http://intercessorsfornigeria.org/?p=10. [sic]

YAHUAH'S PROPHETIC AGENDA

National Prayer Conference Christian Students Social Movement (CSSM 1983)

This year was the year of the coup that ousted the Shagari Government. Yahuah spoke to us as we gathered in prayer in Port Harcourt, not even aware that a coup had taken place. Son of man say to Nigeria; though you have passed through the valley of the shadow of death, thus saith Yahuah, you shall not die but shall live.

At the First National Convention of the Full Gospel Business Men's Fellowship International {FGBMFI} Held at Hotel Presidential in Port Harcourt {1983}

A visiting delegate from New Mexico USA spoke about visions of black men that Yahuah was giving him while he was in his home country. When he asked about who the black men where, Yahuah he said explained to him that these black men were Nigerians. He had never visited Nigeria before and Yahuah told him he will soon take him there because the nation Nigeria was a nation he planned to use in revival. He then spoke on in prophecy. Thus saith Yahuah- Nigeria and Nigerian Christians will be used by Yahuah to preach the gospel in the marketplaces of the World in these last days.

Pastor S. G. Elton spoke prophetically in this meeting concerning two key African nations, saying that Africa is like a gun pointed down. Its turret and muzzle is South Africa. Its trigger is Nigeria. He said the days would come when Apartheid {then at its peak in South Africa} will be removed from South Africa. In those days, he said the Gun of Africa would begin to fire for Yahuah's purpose.

Extract, Tape Recorded Message, West Regional Conference, Ibadan, 24-26/05/07

In 1989, on the way to US, I was in Shrewsbury in UK; I met this accountant who had a message given to him in 1983 during the Rivers of Life Conference in East Anglia in UK. The visioner was in a prayer session with his group when Yahuah began to show him a vision. Yahuah began to show him a vision of countries and lands that was passing through a draught. As he watched, Yahuah brought him over a parcel of territory that typifies Africa. As he looked on, at a particular portion of that land, that portion was in total darkness, sparks of light was shooting out of that darkness while groaning and cries were coming out of that darkness. As he continued to watch, it appeared somebody used a remote control to pause the motion of pictures. At this point he called out to his brethren, he told them that Yahuah was showing him something but it seemed nothing was moving anymore. His friends told him to keep watching while they prayed for him. As soon as they began to pray, it appeared a play button was pressed and the motion came alive again.

Then greater cries were coming out of that land and suddenly there was blinding flash of light that came and swept away that darkness and the whole land birthed with light. Yahuah told him that, that land he had just seen is called Nigeria. Then they now sat down and began to ask themselves the meaning of this vision. And Yahuah told them that Nigeria is a significant nation in His hands for the establishment of His purposes in the last days, to break the sceptre of the religion of sons of the bondwoman, to establish His purposes and that the principality appointed by Lucifer over Nigeria is in the same category as the principality over Israel and European nations. That is as tough as it is going to be to fulfil Yahuah's purposes.

So Yahuah told them {these British brethren} to constitute themselves to be interceding for Nigeria. So when he heard from his friends in 1989, that a Nigerian was coming, he came to see me {Steve} and to handover the responsibility. As he finished the message, he said, since you are a Nigerian, go home and tell your brethren what Yahuah has said. As he finished, he greeted everybody and left.

So it is important to recall what Yahuah has said concerning Nigeria. A land covered with darkness in which there were groaning and cries with sparks of lights but needed a great light from heaven to blow away the darkness. It happened suddenly. It will happen suddenly. {Engr. Steve Olumuyiwa, Narrating}

Ibadan Prayer Conference CSSM {1984}

As we prayed here at a large gathering of many campuses at the Ibadan Polytechnic, Yahuah spoke again during a very deep session of prayers while most of us were on our face on the floor. Yahuah spoke in prophecy saying: My Church in this nation is my hope for the Continent of Africa.

NIGERIA ARISE {*Prophecy, IFN, Core East Regional Conference, Onitsha, 27/1/96*}

Arise Oh Nigeria! Saith Yahuah, Arise from the North, Arise from the South, Arise from the West, Arise from the East. The season of incubation is past. The day to hatch has come and I

Yahuah bring upon you a visitation, my marked visitation. Even though you have not known me, yet I have chosen you. In this day I pass through your land in mercy to renew the face of the nations. Even though the nations are despising you, I have desired you as a place for my glory. Therefore, I Yahuah have jealously watched over you to cause my purpose to be done. I have brought you to the valley of decision. There is no time to waste. Arise as a generation for, I have waited for you. I will desire of you genuine dedication. I Yahuah will make my demands. But I seek to raise out of you a generation of men who will make my glory known in the ends of the earth. I have purposed it, I will do it. But I ask you to arise. Arise in this day; there is no more time to wait. Arise, Arise, from complacency, Arise from ignorance. Know me Yahuah of destiny. Know me Yahuah of covenants. For I seek to exhibit you to the world. I have come this day. Do I desire a commitment from you? I desire not to wait any longer. My time has come and you shall labour in the nations to bring up children. Therefore, arise into this destiny for the world waits for you saith the Spirit of Yahuah.

Arlington Virginia USA ICCC Conference (1996)

At this global Christian convocation of the International Christian Chambers of Commerce (ICCC) held in Arlington VA USA, a white American female delegate called those of us from Nigeria together and intimated us about the word which she said Yahuah spoke to correct her view of Nigeria as a nation that was forsaken by Yahuah. She said that Yahuah said He was preparing Nigeria for use in the end time harvest of souls. She said Yahuah directed her to go read the entire 36th chapter of the book of Ezekiel. He told her that wherever she saw the name Israel in the chapter, she should put the name Nigeria. Yahuah said that way, she will see the full scope of his plan for the nation of Nigeria.

AHOP Conference, Swaziland, 1996

Behold, ye despisers, and wonder, and perish: for I work a work in your days, a work which ye shall in no wise believe, though a man declare it unto you. Acts 13:41.

South Africa, April 2000

Yet it is ten years and I would have changed the face of your continent. For my glory shall come in 10 years.

Behold my servants, in this 10 years I shall need runners, fast runners; they that shall run to and fro in your nations. But where are those runners? For in a short while, the time will come. Therefore, raise runners for me. Send them forth, and I shall bring the continent to a place it will shine

Prophecy received during National Leadership consultation in Lagos on 26th February, 2000 {1040hrs}

I declare I am Yahuah. I ever existed. But my people I declare to you, who has believed my report? Have I not spoken to you in the past? I have declared that I desire your nation as a choice possession to make my name known but your nation has not known me. Your Nation has not stretched out her hands to me. I plead my case against your nation. <u>I bring your nation to the place of a strong cry for there shall be a cry in your nation.</u> These are the days I call you to myself; have I not declared? Do not be forgetful hearers. I plead my case against your nation so they will know me. Review what I have said to you. I assure you, Nigeria will do my will and the nations shall rejoice as Nigeria does my will. I will bring you to the place of acceptability; they will have a pure language; I will put my sickle into your land. I harvest the wicked for judgment. I harvest your nation. The ears that hear will tingle and my Cyrus shall come to lead your nation. Don't despair what will come. I have not left you without a witness. Look to me for direction, says the Spirit of Yahuah.

Yahuah says to Nigeria

I have given you a missionary spirit and am surely going to change the nations of the earth through you. But now I will give you the anointing to change your nation.

Yahuah says, I am going to begin to unravel the corrupt system in Nigeria and men will say it is impossible but I say with Yahuah all things are possible. There is going to be a revival in the Universities and this revival is going to be of such a large magnitude, that the revival in the Universities will affect the secondary schools and will affect the primary schools. And I am going to change Nigeria to the next generation says Yahuah. And Yahuah says the unity of the leaders is coming. It's going to uproot and dethrone the occult. For I'm going to overthrow the occult spirit. <u>And I'm going to use Nigeria to heal the rest of Africa because what happens in Nigeria will affect the whole continent.</u>

Yahuah says I'm going to use the Nigerians in Russia. There will be many churches planted in Russia. Yahuah says I'm going to use your nation. I'm going to use you in the Middle East; Yahuah says I'm getting ready to change many things. I'm getting ready to expose this occult in the highest level. In the next few months, I'm going to tear it down and I'm going to make it shift and there will be day [that] violence will no longer be heard of in the streets of Nigeria. And it will be one of the safest nations on the face of the earth says Yahuah. Halleluiah. Yahuah bless you   (Prophecy by Cindy Jacobs, year 2002)

THE DOORS ARE OPENED (*Pretoria, South Africa, March 18, 2005*)

This is the fifth day of this holy convocation,

I called you from your nations to announce to you that the doors are opened.

For years, ancient doors to the <u>mystery</u> of my grace have been locked to Africa.

By the rebellion and disobedience of your fathers, the doors had been locked.

By their idolatry, bloodshed and immorality, the doors had been locked.

By deception, ignorance and foolishness, the doors have been locked.

But today on this fifth day of your holy convocation,

I Yahuah announce to you that the doors are opened

I have seen your tears.

I have heard the cry of your heart.

I have witnessed your willingness to repent.

I have come to announce to you that the doors are opened to the mystery of Africa.

The doors are opened to the mystery of your life.

Open your eyes carefully and I will show you the doors within THE DOOR.

As you walk into the door of the mystery of Africa,

I will guide you into the mystery of your life.

I Yahuah have come down to make announcement that the doors are open.

My celestial doors are open.

Be careful to know the laws of the heavens.

Be careful to use them to set my dominion on the earth.

My terrestrial doors are open.

I have come to shake the foundations of the earth.

I have come to show you the mysteries of its wealth.

Reach out your hands into the treasures of darkness.

Reach out with MY keys to unlock the hidden riches of secret places.

The doors are opened to the thrones of Africa.

I have come to harvest the souls of kings.

This is the season of their harvest.

I will loose the armour of kings and open to you the gates of their thrones.

The day has come for a continental gathering of kings at the feet of the King of kings.

Open your eyes and you will see the multitudes of doors that are open to you, sons and daughters of Africa.

I have opened doors to the marketplace.

I have opened doors of witty inventions.

I have opened the doors of knowledge and wisdom.

I HAVE OPENED THE DOORS OF POWER

I have opened the doors of prophetic marriages.

Did I not give you the keys to these doors?

Did I not tell you how to open them?

Yet now I have come down to open them myself.

I have released angels into your midst.

They will unlock the ancient doors that have hindered my plans.

They will break the bars of iron.

They will cut them asunder.

I have come to show myself strong.

The doors are open.

Walk in and you will fulfil the <u>mystery</u> of my grace.

ICCC Conference, South Africa (June 2000)

It dawned upon Gunnar Olson, founder of ICCC that it's time for the African nations to rise up and take their rightful place among the nations of the world. He made the following proclamations:

- Africa. this is your Kairos moment, therefore arise and take your destiny

- Africa, be released and accept your divine mandate from heaven

- Africa, your shackles of slavery, poverty, limitations, idolatry, paganism, discrimination, exploitation, servitude, perversion, discord, witchcrafts, ancestral worship, Satanism, and all evil is crushed. Arise, Arise, Arise.

- Africa, bring forth your sons and daughters who will arise and take their rightful place among the kings, princes, and nobles of the earth. Let them execute the righteousness of Yahuah, and advance the purposes of Yahuah to bring healing, prosperity, and manifestations of majesty, excellence, and glory.

- Africa, Yahuah will build a highway of holiness and righteousness, and everyone who walks on this highway will find refuge, strength and purpose

- Africa, all the nations of the earth will come marvel at your wisdom and glory.

- Africa, oh Africa, the deepest fountains and resources of heaven that have been hidden deep in your belly because of the deeds of evil men, are now breaking forth because of the righteous remnants that have regarded the will of Yahuah higher than the opinions of men.

- Africa, Arise, Arise, Arise. For the glory of Yahuah has risen upon you and your enemies are scattered.

VISION RECEIVED BY RON SMITH – PARTICIPATING DELEGATE FROM TEXAS USA AT ICCC NIGERIA NATIONAL CONFERENCE HELD AT EXCELLENCE HOTEL, IKEJA LAGOS ON 12TH MARCH, 1998

While I was praying at the end of Emeka's message, I saw a vision of a Local Africa marketplace. It was looking dingy, dirty and filthy. Then the vision changed. I saw the market transformed into a new environment. Gold, diamond and precious stones of various types were stacked neatly and well arranged on a table. I saw an oil font springing up from the table. I also saw in this new market environment, neatly dressed people in three distinct groups: Men, Boys and Babies (little children).

Then I saw trucks full of gold bars moving across the borders of the countries of Africa. I saw a blood stream flowing ahead of the trucks into villages into which the trucks were coming. As the blood stream entered into the villages, it exploded into white light which enveloped the villages. Thus says Yahuah, There is a wave of prosperity coming from

Yahuah into Africa. The objective is for the salvation of the peoples of Africa. Idolatry will be overthrown in Africa as part of this move. Beware however that you do not replace idolatry with materialism when the release of the wealth comes.

SOMA (Sharing of Ministries Abroad) Conference 2000, South Africa

In summary, Yahuah promised He would change the face of Africa within a decade and that He would do bigger things than were done in the book of the Acts of the Apostles:

There was a time when this was called the Dark Continent; that time is over, says Yahuah, because the light has shone upon you. The light of the Gospel is like a torch of fire that is being lit up by the Holy Spirit in this continent.

This continent will be known in the next ten years, as the continent that reversed the curse of the enemy. Totally reversed the curse and started to walk in the path of blessing. Blessings that will be shone forth to every nation in the world and professionals will look at Africa and will be totally amazed and will stand in awe saying, what happened here? We cannot explain what happened to this continent. There was no possibility. There was no natural possibility whatsoever for this to happen. So everybody will say in this continent, what happened here was not done by human hands, but by the Holy Spirit Himself.

There is an anointing for a miracle, an anointing for the supernatural upon this continent. There is a mantle upon this continent that is a miraculous mantle. It will fall upon anyone who will believe Yahuah, and literally capture the anointing and use it for His glory... there are many, many conquests waiting for men and women, waiting to be conquerors. There are many challenges. There are many, many opportunities. This is the time and land of opportunity for Yahuah's Kingdom.

There will be many, many Kingdom builders because of the anointing of the Holy Spirit. There are many, many men and women of Yahuah, who are waiting for a call from the Almighty, a supernatural kind of call, an anointing of the Holy Spirit. Now, there have been many, many great men of Yahuah who have risen up in the midst of calamity, and anguish, and sorrow, and have shaken there out of their bodies, so to speak, and have travelled all over the world sowing the power of the Almighty Yahuah.

The Holy Spirit says, these men have not been unique. These men have been only the first fruits of what I want to do in Africa, says the Holy Spirit.

Harold Cabelleros went on to say, *I believe the times of miracles are coming to Africa in such a way that will literally overshadow the book of Acts. So many miracles and so powerful miracles, that the shadow of men and women of Yahuah in this continent will heal the sick and raise the dead. It will happen so often that nobody will be amazed anymore when someone gets healed. The supernatural will be the natural thing in this continent ... because the manifestations of the power of the Holy Spirit is growing, and growing, and growing, and growing higher in this continent. Africa will be an exporter of missionaries and prophecies.*

Harold Cabelleros, SOMA Meeting, beyond AD2000, Cape Town South Africa, 2ⁿᵈ Nov.2000
ABOVE ALL, I CALL YOU TO BE INTERCESSORS
(Prophecy from Mount Carmel)
This prophecy was given in 1986 in a Prophetic Conference in Jerusalem, Israel. 153 prophets from 30 to 40 nations had gathered to wait upon and to hear from the Yahuah. The highlights of this prophecy to the entire body of Christ are as follows:

A PROPHECY BY LANCE LAMBERT

It will not be long before there will come upon the world a time of unparalleled upheaval and turmoil. Do not fear for it is I Yahuah who am shaking all things.

I began this shaking with the First World War and I greatly increased it through the Second World War. Since 1973 I have given it an even greater impetus. In the last stage, I plan to complete it with the shaking of the universe itself, with signs in sun and moon and stars.

But before that point is reached, I will judge the nations and the time is near. It will not only be by war and civil war, by anarchy and terrorism, and by monetary collapses that I will judge the nations, but also by natural disasters: by earthquakes, by shortages and famines and by old and new plague diseases. I will also judge them by giving them over to their own ways, the lawlessness, to loveless selfishness, to delusion and to believing a lie; to false religion and an apostate church, even to

Christianity without me. Do not fear when these things begin to happen, for I disclose these things to you before they commence in order that you might be prepared and that in the day of trouble and of evil you may stand firm and overcome.

For I purpose that you may become the means of encouraging and strengthening many who love me but who are weak. I desire that through you many may become strong in me, and that multitudes of others might find my salvation through you.

And hear this! Do not fear the power of the Kremlin, nor the power of the Islamic Revolution, for I plan to break both of them through Israel. I will bring down their pride and their arrogance, and shatter them because they have blasphemed my name. In that day I will avenge the blood of all the martyrs and of the innocent ones whom they have slaughtered. I will surely do this thing for they have thought that there was no one to judge them. But I have seen their ways and I have heard the cries of the oppressed and of the persecuted and I will break their power and make an end of them.

Be ye therefore prepared for when all this comes to pass, to you will be given the great opportunity to preach the Gospel freely to all nations. In the midst of all the turmoil and shaking, and at the heart of everything, is My Church. In the heavenlies she is joined to me in one Spirit and I have destined her for the throne. You who are my beloved, whom I have redeemed and anointed – you are mine.

I will equip and empower you and you will rise up and do great things in My Name, even in the midst of darkness and evil. For I will reveal my power, and my grace and glory through you. Do not hold back nor question My ways with you for in all My dealings with you I have always in mind that you should be part of My Bride and reign with Me. Do not forget that this requires discipline and training. So yield to me that I might do a work in you in the time which is left for I plan even during all this shaking the Bride will make herself ready.

For in the midst of these judgments multitudes upon multitudes will be saved from the nations. You will hardly know how to bring the harvest in, but my Spirit will equip you for the task.

And to Israel, will I also turn in that day, and I will melt the hardening which has befallen her. I will turn their blindness into clear sight, and tear away the veil on their heart. Then shall they be redeemed with heart bursting joy, and it will become a fountain of new and resurrection life to the whole company of the redeemed.

Do not fear for these days, for I have purposed that you shall stand with me and serve me in them. Fear not, for I love you and I will protect you and equip you. I, Yahuah, will anoint you with a new anointing and you will work my works and fulfil My counsel. You shall stand before me, Yahuah of the whole earth and serve Me with understanding and with power and you shall reign with Me during these days. ABOVE ALL, I CALL YOU TO BE INTERCESSORS.

AFRICA AWAKE (By Chad Taylor)

Africa awake to your destiny! For in you is a prophetic seed that is about to break the ground of persecution. From you is coming a tree of righteousness and soundness. Its leaves will be for a shelter for the nations of the earth. For in you is a prophetic seed; an apostolic seed; in you is a corner stone to My last days Church, a pillar in My Temple and a living stone.

Africa awake to your destiny! For in the days to come you will see changes that topple the magistrates and the hierarchy that permits the death of My children. You will see it and be glad. You will say in your hearts Yahuah is gracious and has not forgotten us. The world will report of it and know that Yahuah is in you. The seats of authority will turn; they will turn like water before the face of Yahuah.

Africa awake to your destiny! For your children shall sing a new song! I will break now the curses that have brought drought and famine. Through your children's prayers I will break the chains that hang on your nation's neck. I will loose you from this heavy burden and give you rest. I will unlock the gates of bronze and I will give you the treasures out of darkness says Yahuah.

Africa awake to your destiny! For from you will come a company, a troop, a brigade; they will march with a blazing message of my love! They will march to the steps of destiny and they will bring a Word from Yahuah to the uttermost parts of the earth. From you O Africa will come my generals, and my commanders. From you will come a company of prophets that the earth has yet to see! You will prophesy to the winds of the earth and they will carry the life of my word to the nations.

Africa awake to your destiny. This is your hour of liberation! This is your year of jubilee! Africa awake to your destiny! You will speak my word in this season. You will set in motion these end time events. You will set my house in order. For the seed of prophecy is springing up even now in you, it will shortly bud and bear fruit. It will shortly cast its shadow upon the whole earth, and many shall hear of it and be glad. Africa awaken to your destiny! This is your year of jubilee! (Extract, Prof. Anigbogu's Message, AKBF Continental Conference, 2006)

FELA DUROTOYE at ANCHOR MENS' CONFERENCE FAMILY WORSHIP CENTRE, 2013

YAHUAH spoke to me saying: "By the year 2025, Nigeria will be the most desired destination on earth."

CPSIA information can be obtained
at www.ICGtesting.com
Printed in the USA
BVOW10s0248240817
492934BV00003B/10/P